HOWE SOUND

PORT MELLON

HORSESHOE BAY

GIBSONS

TUWANEK

ROBERTS CREEK

SECHELT

CRET COVE

HALFMOON BAY

STRAIT OF GEORGIA

GRETA GRUNOW GUZEK

The Sunshine Coast

Travellers taking the Langdale ferry to the Sunshine Coast enjoy a
spectacular view of the Brittania Range on the Eastern shore of Howe Sound.

The Sunshine Coast

FROM GIBSONS TO POWELL RIVER

BY HOWARD WHITE

Photography by Keith Thirkell

with Ken Bell, Mary Cain, Paul Galinski, Tim Poole, Tim Turner and Dean vantSchip.

HARBOUR PUBLISHING

CONTENTS

Jervis Inlet is one of the scenic highlights of any visit to the BC coast.

The Sunshine Coast

Desolation Sound north of Powell River, despite the gloomy name given it by Captain Vancouver, offers one of the most enchanting boating experiences in the Pacific Northwest. Here yachts anchor in the tranquil refuge of Prideaux Haven.

UNTIL THE 1980S THE SUB-
limely scenic 100-mile stretch
of shoreline along the eastern
side of Georgia Strait known as the Sunshine
Coast enjoyed a blessed obscurity that allowed its forty-
thousand-odd residents to indulge their oddness to the
fullest. The area has a reputation for being the maverick
among British Columbia's favoured south coast regions
and seems to rejoice in it. In the past twelve provincial elec-
tions, the Sunshine Coast has voted against the government
of the day nine times, a contrariness which has rewarded
the area with some of the twistiest sections of Highway 101
north of Guatemala.

The oddball image works for geography as well as
politics. It's not an island, but you have to take a ferry to get
there—five different ferries if you want to see all of it. Local
developers have spent years dreaming of bridges, tunnels,
overland links and fast commuter ferries aimed at breach-

those who want to preserve the
coast's quiet backwater status provides the spark that animates local politics. At one point in the early 1990s the area
was served by no fewer than nine regularly published newspapers, and still there was never enough room to carry all
the letters to the editor that flare up around such issues as
improving the Westview– Comox ferry service or allowing
the first McDonald's restaurant onto the Sechelt Peninsula.

Being neither fish nor fowl from a geographic stand-
point, the Sunshine Coast lacks some of that romantic aura
that attracted urban hordes to the true islands of the Gulf,
leaving the area to evolve in its own way. Among those in
the know it has long been seen as a haven where people
might do their own thing in their own time with a mini-
mum of interference from the outside world. This has
made it a refuge for painters, writers, hermits, handloggers,
stumpranchers, trappers, prospectors, fishermen, and draft
dodgers of every war since the origi-
nal of the Egmont Jeffries jumped
ship during the 1859 Pig Wars in the
San Juan Islands. They and other
fugitives from the twentieth century
established a string of quiet little villages whose names, from Hopkins
Landing to Secret Cove to Gillies
Bay, reflect their salty sense of self-
possession.

It took until the mid-1980s
for the area's attractions to be discovered in a major way, and by the
early 1990s the Sunshine Coast was
the fourth fastest-growing residential area in BC, to the chagrin of
many of those longtime seekers of
peace and quiet. But it remains one
of the few places within commuting
distance of Vancouver where you
can still experience some of the
sights and scents of the old-time BC
coast of the steamships and the
stumpranches, the float camps and
the fish plants. Villages like Lund

*Government wharves, sturdy steamer docks built of timbers and pilings, were
once the heart of every BC coast community. Westview's combination ferry
slip and boat dock is one of the busiest still in use.*

ing the isolation of the Sunshine Coast while the old-time
residents scheme just as determinedly to preserve it. The
split between those who wish to conjoin with the growth
convulsing BC's Lower Mainland just across the water and

and Pender Harbour still cling to their rocky shorelines like
a fringe of storm-tossed driftwood, connected by red-railed
boardwalks; Gambier and Savary Island children still ride
to school in sea-going schoolbuses; and tide-borne seaweed, shovelled into gunny bags and wheeled up the beach
trail in the wheelbarrow, is still the fertilizer of choice for
home vegetable gardens throughout the region.

PARTS OF THE SUNSHINE COAST HAVE ENJOYED their own separate renown for decades.

The city of Powell River at the northern end of the territory, still the largest single community in the region, has been a destination for ocean-going ships since the world's largest pulp and paper mill was built there on the world's shortest river in 1910.

Nearby Desolation Sound has been known to discriminating boaters as one of the Pacific Northwest's most enchanting cruising experiences since Capi Blanchet immortalized it in her 1950s yachting classic, *The Curve of Time*. The feature attraction is an enchanted maze of islands and lagoons called Prideaux Haven, which by the 1980s had become the most popular marine park in the province.

Jervis Inlet, a mountain-girt fifty-mile-long fjord that cleaves the Sunshine Coast into north and south sections of roughly equal mass and population, has been a must-see for travellers of the world for generations. Princess Louisa Inlet, a canyon-like offshoot near the head of Jervis, attracted the likes of John Barrymore and Andrew Carnegie, who paid homage to its fabled mile-high splendour back in the early years of the century.

Just to the south, Skookumchuck Rapids at the entrance to Sechelt Inlet has graduated into legend as one of North America's most awesome saltwater cataracts, the sea-going graveyard of dozens of unwary small boaters. Both scenic wonders have thankfully been preserved as parks, though not before the north side of the Skookumchuck was transformed into a giant open-pit gravel mine. Timber companies continue to gnaw at the forest around Princess Louisa, rather in the spirit of old-time Athens businessmen grinding up the Parthenon to make cement (Gotta keep the boys busy).

Pender Harbour, an eccentric fishing community built around a jigsaw puzzle of coves, reefs and sloughs where some people still do their Saturday shopping in small motorized "kicker" boats, has long been known as "The Venice of the North," and once served as the bustling winter capital of the populous Sechelt Indian nation.

Anchoring the southern end of the Sunshine Coast, the town of Gibsons (I still like to call it Gibsons Landing, though it deep-sixed the "Landing" in 1947) boasts per-

The once-ubiquitous Union Steamships passenger freighters are but a fond memory, but Sunshine Coasters still depend on ships of the BC Ferries fleet. Here the Queen of Cowichan approaches Langdale.

haps the west coast's most familiar sea front. It was imprinted on millions of minds all over the globe during its nineteen years as the setting of the popular CBC television drama *The Beachcombers*.

BEGINNINGS

YOU MIGHT THINK THE SCENIC ATTRACTIONS alone would have sparked a more general interest in the Sunshine Coast, but a full century elapsed between the beginnings of European settlement in the late nineteenth century and the boom of the 1990s.

Non-Indian history on the Sunshine Coast began with the arrival of the Spanish explorer Jose Maria Narvaez in 1789 followed in 1790 by an English expedition under Captain George Vancouver. Both churned through the territory in such a panic to find the fabled Northwest Passage they failed to notice Sechelt Inlet, Pender Harbour and a host of other major geographical features. They did find time, however, to replace the poetic and myth-laden Indian names which had served to identify the area's islands and inlets for thousands of years with the names of minor naval officials, school chums, mistresses, etc. The names for Thormanby Islands, Merry Island, Buccaneer Bay, Epsom Point, and Derby Point were inspired by an English horse race.

In other areas, southern Vancouver Island for instance, Indian names were widely adopted by the new settlers and today give a special flavour to the area— Saanich, Malahat, Cowichan, Nanaimo. Sharkain, Chichatomos, Tsawcome—names that reflected the Sechelt's long and intimate relationship with the geography of the Sunshine Coast, are all but lost. Apart from some less prominent geographical sites such as Sakinaw Lake near Pender Harbour and Clowhom Lakes up Salmon Inlet, the only major Sechelt name to survive is Sechelt itself, although "Sechelt" was not originally a place name, but rather the name of the shíshálh people themselves.

Over the years more explorers came to fill in the blanks left in the charts by Vancouver and Narvaez— George Richards in 1860 and Daniel Pender in 1863, but no settlers followed in their wakes until the late 1880s. By then, the arrival of the trans-continental railway in Vancouver, and the Pre-Emption Act of 1884, which made it easier to obtain Crown land, had shifted BC development into high gear. Sechelt was the site of one of the first attempts by a European to take up land for settlement on the Sunshine Coast when John Scales, a decommissioned Royal Engineer fresh from building the Cariboo wagon road, was awarded a 260-acre homestead there in 1869. But the preemption lay unoccupied until it was purchased by Sechelt's first real non-Indian settler, Thomas John Cook. Cook and his family didn't get established until 1890, about the time other settlers were staking out waterfront preemptions all along the Sunshine Coast from Port Mellon to Prideaux Haven.

Up on Texada Island things began stirring a little earlier when the BC premier of the day, Amor de Cosmos (a.k.a. Bill Smith), jointly purchased 50,000 acres for development as an iron mine in 1874. De Cosmos was forced to resign in the ensuing scandal, but eventually the iron mine did get up and running, providing the Sunshine Coast with its first two towns. The twin cities of Van Anda and Texada City boasted "three hotels and saloons, a hospital, a variety of stores and businesses, a local newspaper (*The Coast Miner*), a jail, and an opera house." The mine fizzled out in 1916, but other mines and businesses intent on exploiting Texada's immense limestone and mineral deposits kept the community alive.

CHRONICLES OF NON-INDIAN SETTLEMENT ON the lower Sunshine Coast usually begin with the story of George Gibson, a gangling British naval officer who took out the first preemption in what would become Gibsons Landing in 1886, but I have never found old George had much to recommend him except the fact he somehow managed to wash up on these shores before most anybody else of the non-Indian persuasion. Dour and stolid, he always struck me as an unfortunate person to erect a founding myth upon.

My candidate for Founding Spirit of the Sunshine Coast is Harry Roberts, the patron saint of Roberts Creek, who didn't arrive until 1900 but was much more the classic Sunshine Coast personality than Gibson. Imaginative, visionary, non-conforming to a fault—he literally put the Sunshine Coast on the map. An art student in England and later a painter, author and homespun philosopher, Roberts was the first Sunshine Coast pioneer to put into practice the idea that there are other things to do here just as important as cutting the trees, catching the fish, and doing the developments. But he also forged a bit of an industrial empire around Roberts Creek between the turn of the century and 1930. He even built himself a castle, albeit a wooden one. Then he

chucked it and took to sea in his trusty yawl the *Chack-Chack* where he could paint, write and philosophize full time, eventually resettling on a paradisical south-facing beach at Cape Cockburn on Nelson Island. There he constructed his celebrated second home, "Sunray," raised his three children, and kept house with his second and third wives, give or take.

Sunshine Coast pioneer Jim Spilsbury tells a story about Harry during his Sunray days that provides a glimpse of his uncommon character. For years Spilsbury and his wife Win summered on a choice piece of waterfront on Ballet Bay near Cape Cockburn which they had purchased from a crusty Norwegian boatbuilder named Sandvold. Sandvold was a bachelor, but not quite a confirmed one, it would seem. During the time in question, Harry Roberts felt called upon to take long absences from his wife Cherry in order to beachcomb, trade, paint, philosophize, philander—Harry himself never knew quite what he was up to at any given moment. Cherry had apparently quit caring and had taken to relieving her loneliness by entertaining Sandvold. Something tipped Harry off, so he pretended to leave on a trip but anchored in Quarry Bay and doubled back through the bush in time to catch Sandvold docking his fishboat at the Roberts dock in Cockburn Bay. Confirming his worst suspicions by peeping through the bedroom window, Harry considered his situation. He was wiry enough, but a flyweight. He weighed maybe 140 pounds soaking wet, while his rival was in the 200 range. Irate as he was, our Harry was no fool. He retreated quietly up the path and made his way over the hill to the dock, where he stepped aboard Sandvold's boat—and climbed up the rigging. When the big Norwegian came tromping down the gangplank in the wee hours of the morning, whistling and looking quite pleased with himself, Harry took a flying leap and landed on his adversary's head. Before Sandvold knew what hit him, Harry was all over him, thrashing him senseless with a cod bonker and cutting his boat adrift on the tide. Sandvold eventually recovered and had the bad grace to charge Harry with assault. When they appeared before the redoubtable magistrate William "Judge" Parkin in Powell River, Parkin listened as Sandvold began relating his complaint, frowned, then interrupted.

"Do you mean to stand there and tell me a strapping great oaf like *you* needs this court's help to protect you from a puny little runt like *him*?"

"He yoomp! He yoomp from de sky, your highness..."

"Case dismissed!"

Above: Harry Roberts in 1910.

Above: "This clearing bought by the years of his labour is being repossessed...the walls of green are closing in," wrote author Hubert Evans in "Pioneer O Pioneer." Many coastal homesteads, like Harry Roberts' charming "Sunray" on Nelson Island, were abandoned when first-generation settlers passed on.

Left: Night shift at the Powell River pulp and paper mill, still one of the largest in Canada.

The Sunshine Coast has served as a holiday playground for generations of Vancouver youngsters. These boys make the most of a glorious summer day by plunging off the Vaucroft dock on Thormanby Island.

HARRY WAS TYPICAL OF THE SLIGHTLY OFF-centre types who sifted over the hills and fetched up like continental driftwood here at the ocean's edge because they were too haywire to fit in more organized portions of the globe, but that is not the only reason I nominate him as the area's chief historical mascot. It was Harry's fertile brain that hatched the idea of combining all the coast's isolated settlements and landmarks under one regional name-tag so that in future, TV weathermen would have something to call the part of the province that remained after they'd listed off the Yukon and Southern Lakes, the North

Coast, Cariboo, Columbia River, Vancouver Island, Lower Mainland, etc. Actually he gives the credit to his granny, Charlotte Roberts, who came out to the coast in 1890 to enjoy her sunset years, thereby launching another of the area's traditions as a retirement area. Granny Roberts, so Harry claimed, first began referring to the little strip of coast around The Creek as "the Sunshine Belt." But Harry it was who undertook to emblazon the slogan in foot-high letters across the wall of the freight shed on the Roberts Creek steamer dock—this was after he'd given up badgering the federal government to build a steamer dock in Roberts

Creek, and rallied the local lads to build one themselves.

After Harry decided he'd created a bit of a monster and fled the unbearable hurly-burly of Roberts Creek in 1929, less imaginative promoters continued to exploit his brainwave, changing the arid-sounding "Belt" to the saltier "Coast" and extending its reach until by 1951 when Blackball Ferries linked the Pender Harbour–Gibsons road into the Pacific Coast Highway, the "Sunshine Coast" reached all the way from Port Mellon to Egmont. In recent years it has been something of a surprise to south-enders to look around and discover their northern neighbours on the Powell River side of Jervis Inlet also setting up housekeeping inside the Sunshine Coast tent. This unilateral extension of the territory is not without biogeoclimatic justification, as we shall see, but it raises certain questions.

The most recent gerrymandering of BC's electoral districts in 1989 placed the two areas together in one constituency called "Powell River–Sunshine Coast." This would seem to indicate that the provincial government views Powell River and the Sunshine Coast as two separate entities. Indeed, treating them as one immediately creates a new naming problem: how do you distinguish the two quite distinct centres of population from each other? Having to get your mouth around "Upper Sunshine Coast" and "Lower Sunshine Coast" every time you want to evoke Powell River or the original Sunshine Coast complicates life unnecessarily. Powell Riverites have solved the matter to their own satisfaction simply by removing any reference to sunshine from the southern territory and re-dubbing it "The Peninsula" (pronounced pen-int-shoe-la). They are not troubled by the geographical fact that only half the area referred to is located on the actual Sechelt Peninsula. Occupants of the lower Sunshine Coast, not eager to be known as a lower form of anything, deal with the problem by ignoring northern pretensions to sunshiny status, invariably referring to any waypoint along the forty-mile stretch between Saltery Bay and Bliss Landing simply as "Powell River." Although it does not seem to have occurred to anyone on the Lower Sunshine Coast Board of Trade, the obvious solution would be to invoke the area's first European explorers, the ones who left such place names as *Texada*

Like other parts of the Pacific Northwest, the Sunshine Coast is home to heated debate between pro-logging and anti-logging groups. Here a logging company entertains elementary school children on a field trip.

Island and *Malaspina* Strait, and replace the English word "lower" with its Spanish equivalent, *baja*, which is free of pejorative undertones. The *Baja* Sunshine Coast, which local usage would shorten to *The Baja*, would restore to the southern side a clear lead in the drive for vacationland ambiance.

Even without this recent complication, it would be pointless to deny that the name "Sunshine Coast" has been the target of a certain amount of jeering and ridicule over the years, especially by visitors who inadvertently come to sample the promised sunshine during the monsoon season, which can last from October to May, and has been known to include July and August. The place is located in a temperate rainforest, after all.

Whatever claim to legitimacy the Sunshine name may have, I make a poor champion of it, having once started a publication called *Raincoast Chronicles* which was quite outspokenly dedicated to projecting a more authentically mist-shrouded, rainswept image for the region. True, geographers have included the original Sunshine Belt, from Gower Point north, in the more benign Gulf Island biogeoclimatic zone (Gibsons was left in the dreary Coastal Western Hemlock zone), but it is clearly on the moist edge of the zone. According to Earl Coatta, a meteorologist at the Atmospheric Environmental Services in Vancouver, the average sunshine total at Merry Island Lightstation off Halfmoon Bay is 1,873 hours per year, slightly better than downtown Vancouver's 1,818 hours, but well below Victoria's 2,185 hours and the provincial high, Cranbrook's 2,229 hours. Precipitation records tell the same tale. Sechelt's average rainfall of 42 inches is closer to Vancouver's 48 inches than Victoria's 25 inches.

Harry Roberts wasn't the only pioneer to woo tourists by trumping up claims of microclimatic anomaly. Forty miles to the west, the Ashworth family attempted to lure unsuspecting customers to the "Royal Savary Hotel," their rustic lodge on Savary Island, by calling it a "South Sea Island Paradise." Captain G.J. Ashworth, another backwoods visionary who had much to do with establishing Savary as the coast's busiest summer cottage centre way back in the 1920s, even induced his son Bill to greet visitors in a grass skirt and lei, a gimmick which produced mixed results given the younger Ashworth's Ichabod Crane-like physique. On the Powell River shore just a few miles south of Savary, local imagination took an even bolder flight in naming a stretch of sandy shoreline "Palm Beach," later the site of BC's longest running folk festival. Interestingly enough, science lends more credence to the climatic claims of the Ashworth family than those of the Roberts. Just around the corner from Savary, Pendrell Sound on Little Redonda Island has long been known to mariculturists as the only place on the coast where sea water is warm enough to inspire Japanese oysters to spawn on a regular basis. The coastal edge of the Powell River district, from Savary south, shares the same favoured Gulf Island climatic characteristics as the Pender Harbour-to-Gibsons coastline, with one exception. According to *The Atlas Of British Columbia*, there is a pinhole in the provincial climatic map which places Savary Island and a fringe of mainland shore from just south of Palm Beach to Desolation Sound as well as Big Redonda Island in a special category that has higher summer temperatures (18-20°C daily mean) than any other part of the BC coast.

LOAFERS AND MUCKERS

BACK IN THE 1980S, BIG AL DAVIDSON (A.K.A. "The Mouth That Roared"), a Vancouver sportscaster who bought the old Cecil Reid place in Pender Harbour, earned himself a black footnote in Sunshine Coast history by announcing on air that the people of the region were nothing but deadbeats and welfare bums. Meaningful glances passed around the waterfront when two charter boats belonging to the pint-sized jock-sniffer went up in flames several months later—and the Mighty Mouth himself was charged with arson. Smug as we felt on that occasion, it must be admitted that Davidson was not the first outlander to be mystified by what appears to be an extensive community just kind of floating in the salt mist with no economic pillars holding it up.

THIS IS LESS THE CASE IN POWELL RIVER, WHERE the smokestacks of what was once the world's largest pulp and paper mill still dominate the skyline, and the Texada skyline just across the strait is terraced by limerock quarries. Down the coast at Port Mellon near Gibsons, Howe Sound Pulp and Paper operates a smaller, more modern pulp mill. Still, between them these two mills only employ 1,500 people, which leaves about 25,000 voting-age residents unaccounted for. What do they do?

According to the area's economic development offices, 18.5 percent of the Sunshine Coast's work force is employed by the forest industry, either as loggers or mill-workers. The next largest resource industry is fishing, a long way back at 1.9 percent. The service industries make up by far the largest block of jobs, employing over 60 percent of

Grief Point light, a Powell River landmark, is captured in this evocative watercolour by local artist April White, a descendant of the famous Haida carver Charles Edenshaw.

the work force. This is not necessarily a reflection of tourist activity, which involves only about 10 percent. Unemployment is chronically high, hovering in the 20 percent range.

I can hear the ghost of Al Davidson drumming its fingers. There's a hell of a lot of people who don't fit readily into any StatsCan job category, I admit, but this still doesn't give credence to the welfare bums rap. I'm afraid the only way to explain is to delve into some abstract metaphysics.

It's true that the Sunshine Coast, by virtue of being an oddball sort of place, attracted oddball sorts of people—but oddballishness is not in itself a very precise category. You can be an oddball by being too fat or too thin, too bright or too dull, too hyper or too sluggish. The motley crew that populated the coast over the past few centuries included examples of all these ilks and more. Even the Indians had the gentle Dominick Charlie who wished to do nothing but dance, and the psychotic Ts'kahl who

would kill you just for being in his way. Later came people like Mac Macdonald, who used gorgeous Princess Louisa Inlet as a stage for expounding his creed of loaferdom, and others like Powell River's non-stop entrepreneur Emil Gordon, who considered the day wasted unless he launched at least one unlikely new enterprise.

But amid all this variety you can discern two broad types, two pioneer strains who can be distinguished from each other by their reason for being on the Sunshine Coast. The first are those who came here for love of the place and were indifferent to the economic prospects, and the second are those who came here for economic reasons—to make a living or a fortune—and were indifferent to the *placeness* of the place.

For argument's sake let's use Princess Louisa Mac's term and call the first group the loafers—keeping in mind the fine art of loafing can require a good deal of concerted effort. The second group let's call the muckers, because they tend to be always mucking away at piles of trees or fish or

*A family takes advantage of the soft sands and welcoming waters at lovely
Porpoise Bay Park on Sechelt Inlet.*

rocks, even though they will tell you the only reason they do it is to get rich enough to retire and enjoy the finer things in life—exactly what the loafers do, except the loafers do it directly and the muckers put it off. Despite this apparent agreement on ultimate aims, you can dip into coast history at any juncture and find the two factions working determinedly at cross-purposes and denouncing each other in the letters columns.

The muckers include most of the loggers and mill-workers as well as a good many of the original fishing families, who were brought in to provide labour for the salteries and canneries. They especially include the entrepreneurs and developers, like Herbert Whittaker, who gazed upon the pristine wilderness around Sechelt in 1895 and saw the makings of a private fiefdom, and Thomas Hamilton, the multimillionaire inventor who was so affected by the scenic splendour of Princess Louisa Inlet in 1940 he couldn't rest until he'd devised a way to get it generating revenue.

My family were muckers. We ended up on the coast because my father had the opportunity, back in 1950, to take over a small logging camp at Green Bay on Nelson Island. When that played out he found something else close by. It was an easy place to get by in if you weren't too choosey about what you did, and as the settlements grew Dad operated the area's first sand and gravel business, built one of its first gas stations, and ran the town waterworks. For years we all had the feeling it was an unfortunate accident we had become Sunshine Coasters, figuring if we'd played our cards right we could be in a place with a healthier payroll, like Nanaimo or Campbell River. I was brought up with the impression it was really all happening somewhere else, and if I had any brains I should use them to get away to one of those places at the first opportunity. That was typical of the element who followed jobs to the area. This strain tends to support clearcut logging and wide-open development while showing less concern for the preservation of rural values, although I am living proof that the longer anyone stays, the more his motives tend to get confused.

The loafer tradition was typified by Harry Roberts, who would have fought to the death anybody who tried to push him off his quarter section of paradise on Nelson Island, and by his friend Hubert Evans, the Quaker author of *Mist On The River* and *O Time In Your Flight*, who ended years of questing by settling on an acre of beachfront at Roberts Creek in 1928. Another was Bertrand Sinclair, the high-rolling western writer who cowboyed in Montana and hung out on the Barbary Coast before sinking roots at Pender Harbour in 1920. Alan and Sharie Farrell, the coast's ultimate boat people, subsisted for fifty years by squatting on the beach and building exquisite boats from driftwood, living in them for a few years, making the odd crossing to Hawaii or Tahiti, then selling them and

building new ones—fifty-two in all. (Alan's son Barrie, as designer of the most popular commercial fish-boat hull on the BC coast, was responsible for placing an even greater number of hulls in coastal waters.) People like the Sinclairs, the Macdonalds and the Farrells had seen the world and chose to settle on the Sunshine Coast because its inspiring setting and quiet ways let them get down to the serious business of milking their days here on earth for the most satisfaction possible. Loafing in the Macdonald tradition carries no connotation of laziness, since they could be quite industrious in extracting the manifold satisfactions the coast has to offer. Their heirs tend to be fiercely protective of the region's traditional qualities, its peaceful country spaces, unspoiled waters and leisurely pace.

In true Sunshine Coast fashion, I'm taking a long time to make a simple point: the type of people described above do not require smokestack industry to survive. They've got the main thing they want in life already—the place of their dreams. For that they are willing to do without a lot of consumer goods considered necessary to life in most of the western world, which allows them to do without the income normally used to buy such goods. My friend Sammy Lamont used to say all he needed to get by was $500 cash for some flour, tea and diesel. This was not back in the dirty thirties, and Sammy was no hermit living in a hollow stump. He and his partner Ann Clemence spent the winters in a fine waterfront home in Pender Harbour and the summers cruising the upper coast in their commodious sailboat, the *Kivak*. And no, Sam wasn't landed gentry or a retired banker. He grew up in a cedar shack in the bush behind Powell River and spent most of his working years as a beachcomber salvaging escaped sawlogs. Ann is an ex-nurse trained in England. The two of them didn't want for much. Their furniture was of the finest solid wood construction—all made by Sam himself. They ate well from the sea and from their seaweed-rich vegetable garden, fresh in the summer and put up as preserves in winter. They had tons of friends. They spent their days exploring some of the most dramatic landscape in the world. They lived great lives, and they worked hard for it, but not in a pulp mill. To Statistics Canada they were loafers.

To a greater or lesser degree, many Sunshine Coasters fit the same pattern. This certainly applies to the coast's many artists, writers, musicians and craftspeople, many of whom supplement their sales by working as part-time gardeners, carpenters, marijuana ranchers or bulldozer drivers. Few have achieved such perfect independence as Sam and Ann or Alan and Sharie, but piecing together a livelihood by being handy and living well far below the poverty line is a grand tradition on the Sunshine Coast.

Part One

The Gibsons Area

Sunrise on Gibsons harbour. Gibsons was founded by a man who set out in a small boat looking for property and it has been a magnet for boaters ever since.

WHEN MY DAD AND I rode on the ceremonial first sailing of the auto ferry across Howe Sound in 1951, we boarded a shimmying cast-off from Puget Sound called the *MV Quillayute*. It docked at the government wharf in Gibsons, which was very handy but caused gridlock in Gibsons' infamous six-way intersection even then. Some years later the ferry corporation revealed its penchant for locating terminae in non-places and relocated the Sunshine Coast base to a desolate stretch of beach near Langdale Creek, four miles north of Gibsons, where it has remained since.

The hard life of the pioneer shows in the faces of George and Charlotte Gibsons, founders of Gibsons Landing. Their dog, on the other hand, seems to have the best of all possible worlds.

About 99.9 percent of all the cars unloading at the Langdale dock take the centre and left lanes to Gibsons and points north. The other .1 percent turn right toward Port Mellon. The whole lower ten-mile section of the Sunshine Coast Highway, which is actually set apart with its own name—the Port Mellon Highway—shivers in the shadow of Mount Elphinstone and offers little to the traveller but a view of the coast's industrial underbelly. On the other hand a trip along the Port Mellon Highway goes far toward answering the question about what coast folk do. Along the way you pass the area's last significant sawmill, a played-out gravel pit local government hopes will someday become a busy industrial park, and several of the large "log-sorts" that make Howe Sound the world's largest log booming and sorting ground. About 75 percent of the BC coast's annual 30-million-cubic-metre timber harvest is brought here to be graded, parcelled up and re-shipped to the mills of the Lower Mainland. It is the spillage from this traditional Howe Sound activity that gave rise to the Gibsons area's fabled community of beachcombers, or as they now prefer to be known, "log salvors." The one dramatic event you can sometimes observe along this route is one of the elephantine self-dumping log barges in the act of relieving itself of its load. They come down from up the coast piled high with enough logs to build all the houses in a good-sized town, and flood the bilges on one side, causing the vessel to heel over until the mountain of wood tumbles off and the vessel pops out sideways with a Niagara-like commotion. It is one of the visual cliches of coast life which, like the spawning of the salmon, still makes you catch your breath the first few times you encounter it for real.

At the end of the Port Mellon Highway is Port Mellon, site of BC's longest-surviving pulp and paper mill, established in 1908 by a Victorian adventurer with an admirable flowing beard named Captain Henry Augustus Mellon. The grumpy old salt promptly went broke, but not before he laid one of the foundation stones of the BC economy by successfully producing the province's first sheet of authentic wood-fibre pulp. His erstwhile enterprise eventually revived under different ownership, then went broke again, and continued to stop and start under various owners until being taken over in 1951 by BC's second largest forest products company, Canadian Forest Products. In 1988 CanFor partnered with Oji Paper of Japan to transform Port Mellon into one of the most modern mills in Canada. Although the upgrade added a newsprint line and doubled the mill's daily output from 500 to 1,000 tons, it cleverly managed to do so without adding significantly to the existing payroll of 500 persons—which still makes it the largest single employer on the *Baja* Sunshine Coast.

Visitors to the newly reborn Howe Sound Pulp and Paper expecting to find hordes of brutes massaging the works with six-foot spanners and balancing over burbling vats of bone-melting caustic will be struck by an eerily deserted air about the place. The mighty engines hum robotically along, guided only by scattered pockets of workers slumped at computer terminals in soundproof cubicles equipped with air conditioning and exer-cycles.

At one time Port Mellon supported a substantial company townsite resplendent with restaurant, community hall and even a hotel—the Seaside—located on the banks of the Sunshine Coast's most poetically named watercourse, the Rainy River. The highlight of old Port Mellon's social season was Labour Day, topped off by the crowning of the Pulp Queen. This would be followed by the Pulp Ball, during which numbers of attendees would celebrate by attempting to beat each other to pulp. Most townsite residents made their grateful escape when the road was punched through to Gibsons in 1954, but the company kept some houses in service for new arrivals and management until the early 1980s. The last of these was demolished in 1988, leaving only the renegade private townsite half a mile west of the mill, still officially known to the world as Dogpatch.

Founded in 1908, the Port Mellon pulp mill was one of the first on the coast, but upgrading made it also one of the most modern mills in the province in the 1990s.

Masochists who take this less travelled road may be overcome by the gloom of the landscape and despair for people who voluntarily accept life sentences to such purgatorial surroundings. I have often harboured similar thoughts, passing through industrial backwaters like Aberdeen, Washington—but to do so is to presume too much. Just as the soot-caked rowhouses of Nottingham produced one of the century's most visionary glorifiers of the sheer joy of living in D.H. Lawrence, and Aberdeen gave birth to the rock prophet Kurt Cobain, bleak Port Mellon will long be remarked as the gestation-place of Peter Trower, the poetic genius who penned such inspirational anthems to coastal existence as "The Alders" and "Along Green Tunnels." In his poem "When The Mill Was

Our Mother" Trower reveals a bit of what old Port Mellon felt like to the inmates:

When the mill was our mother...
an uncouth mother
of belching stacks and old machinery...
who deeded us a town to live in
tumbledown without pretensions
on the rainy river's brink
full of tarpaper palaces
with pulp-lined interiors
full of simple caring people...
Like one family we lived...
in that kingdom of friendly destiny
we had nothing we had everything

Battling depression brought on by industrial squalor wherever it's found, it can be useful to think of Pete and his comrades taking sulfurous succour from the old Port Mellon mill, keeping the flame burning perhaps a little brighter against the gloom of their surroundings.

THE 99.9 PERCENT who resist the urge to turn right coming off the ferry need not trouble themselves with such existential perplexities. The three-mile drive into Gibsons Landing passes above some of the better beaches on the lower coast—most of them used only by the choice waterfront homes that front them, although there are some well-concealed public access points. The whole of the lower Sunshine Coast, including Gambier and Keats islands, Sechelt Inlet and Jervis Inlet, is infested with summer camps; the YMCA, the Boy Scouts, the Girl Guides, and every church in the phone book have nice spreads. One of the humbler installations, the Salvation Army's Camp Sunrise, can be seen from the highway just past the Langdale ferry terminal.

Before reaching Gibsons Landing the traveller passes two lesser landings, Hopkins and Granthams. Most people who don't live there can't tell you which is which, so remember: Hopkins is just a hop from the ferry and the two G-landings, Granthams and Gibsons, are side by side at the farther end of the twisty little drive. What is note-

The old liquor store in Gibsons became one of the most recognizable buildings in Canada after the CBC television selected it for the set of their adventure series "The Beachcombers."

worthy about these communities including the part of Gibsons nearest them is how many of the older structures—the original Mansard-roofed Granthams store as well as the millworkers' bungalows, summer cottages and many of the sagging commercial buildings of the old First War Gibsons core—have managed to survive, preserving the quaint old fishing village flavour that has made Gibsons such a favourite among Sunday painters and calendar publishers, not to mention the movie industry. It's a minor miracle which must have the town's condo developers wondering what they did wrong.

When Philip Keatley, the Canadian Broadcasting Corporation producer who originated the *Beachcombers* TV series, phoned me for advice on where to find a coastal village authentic enough to serve as the location for the show, I spoke against Gibsons because I thought the original look of the place was too far gone even then, way back in the early 1970s. I told him he should take his show up the road to Egmont, which was a more unspoiled example of the traditional BC fishing village. A lot of people have reason to be grateful he ignored my counsel, since the *Beachcombers*, filmed in Gibsons, went on to enjoy a 19-year run as the most successful television drama ever produced in Canada, while a later show called *Ritter's Cove*, which Keatley did locate in Egmont, bombed after a few seasons.

Even though the last *Beachcombers* episode was filmed in 1992, reruns perpetuate it almost everywhere except Canada. Some first-time visitors still steam up their windscreens and lose control of their Winnebagos as they swing into lower Gibsons and without any warning find themselves smack in the middle of the hallowed *Beachcombers* set.

"Good gawd Martha, look! There's Molly's Reach right there staring at us!"

"And Smitty's marina over there!"

"Hey Mom, I think I see Relic's boat!"

"Can we stop and look, Daddy? Puh-leeeze!"

What is especially beguiling to visitors is that the town itself does so little to advertise or acknowledge its connection to TV-land, leaving them to discover it on their own—if they can find a place to park the camper without coming to grief in the coast's most accident-prone six-way intersection. All summer long you can find tourists peering with cupped hands through the windows of the old liquor store, which the CBC turned into a stage cafe known to millions as Molly's Reach. For many years, the most interesting thing to be seen in the false-fronted old store was a prodigious display of rat droppings.

One summer an enterprising type tried to set up a real-life cafe offering Molly's famous homemade pie and the Relic Special (ketchup on everything), set off with a display of *Beachcombers* memorabilia, but the village wouldn't give her a parking permit for the vacant Reach. Harry Smith, the owner of the building, tried to start a restaurant on the premises again in 1995. The town council responded by saying they didn't want to be rushed into anything, before finally bowing to public outrage and backing down. Any other town in the universe would have bronzed the *Persephone*, the beachcombing tug operated by series hero Nick Adonidas (played by the late Bruno Gerussi), and mounted it in Pioneer Square, surrounded by fibreglass replicas of the entire Beachcomber cast, but Gibsons shrugs and goes about its life, glad the traffic stoppages caused by outdoor shooting are finally over.

Clearly, this town of 6,000 is not about to be swept off its feet by a little cinematic glitter. On the contrary, the longer the series went on, the more the CBC seemed to fall under the influence of Gibsons. After living in the village for several seasons the film cowboys began to realize the life around them offered much richer material than the cheesy fantasies they parachuted in from Toronto, and began producing episodes more reflective of actual coastal experience. Locals hired as go-fers and extras gradually took on more important roles, like my old DeMolay brother Johnny Smith, a real-life beachcomber who went from boat handler to director, and is now jet-setting around the globe as a film producer. Others, like Gerussi, downshifted from the fast lane to stay on as permanent Sunshine Coast residents, abetted not a little by the booty from nineteen years of pretend beachcombing. Legend has it the mighty Nick piloted the *Persephone* through a generation of high-seas high jinks twisting on a helm that wasn't actually connected to anything, the real operator huddling out of view in the bilge. Largely as a result of the long run of the *Beachcombers*, the Gibsons–Roberts Creek area has a higher concentration of retired and semi-retired film types than any precinct north of Marin County. It has also served as the setting for Stephen King's horror film *Needful Things* and the film version of L.R. Wright's Sechelt murder mystery *The Suspect*.

This is what I like about Gibsons. It has its feet planted firmly on the ground. It has a long history of seriousness which it is not about to toss away just to become a world-famous movie capital. It would be hard to think of a more serious individual than old George Gibson, the man who made his storied landing on the Gibsons beach in 1886, unless it was his wife, Charlotte. Just glancing at the portrait of them standing in front of their rustic homestead after twenty years of roughing it in the bush with their numerous offspring is to be dosed with enough grimness to last the average person a good month. Old George's sad baggy eyes and stooping shoulders, his wife's downturned mouth and forbidding stare go well beyond

"American Gothic" into something like "Canadian To-Hell-With-It."

Like George Gibson, who came to the coast after a career as a British naval officer, many early settlers of the Howe Sound area were staid WASPs on the verge of retirement. George Hopkins, who in 1906 bought the 160-acre site that would become Hopkins Landing, was a British engineer who'd sold his Swansea boiler works for health reasons. George Grantham of Granthams Landing was an eminent Vancouver businessman who bought 800 feet of waterfront on Howe Sound because he wanted someplace to stick a summer cabin and in 1909 that was the smallest parcel he could buy. He never actually lived full time at the village that took his name.

These firstcomers manifested some behaviourisms that present-day residents probably consider unique to their own times. Many of them came from the city seeking escape and many subsequently found it necessary, as Lester Peterson remarked in *The Gibsons Landing Story*, to "shuttle back and forth between West Howe Sound and Vancouver, seeking employment in Vancouver to keep the wolf from the door at home." The founders no doubt viewed this survival tactic as a temporary measure soon to be eliminated by an expanding local economy. They might be surprised to return today and see the vast battalion of commuters hugging insulated mugs and massaging laptops as they wait to pile aboard the 6:20 ferry at Langdale each morning.

The 360-car C-class ferry Queen of Cowichan *is readied for the early morning commuter run at the Langdale dock.*

When the enterprising F. C. Grantham began laying water pipes and surveying his 800 feet of paradise into small lots five years before the First World War, he probably didn't realize he was trailblazing a subdividing and selling impulse that would preoccupy peninsula people increasingly for the rest of the century. Sometimes it seems as if every other tree on the Sunshine Coast has a For Sale sign on it, and few are the residents who haven't traded property up, down or sideways at least once. Some properties have been bought and sold so many times it is claimed they've generated more in sales commissions than they're worth to buy.

An event transpired in 1905 that greatly aided Gibsons' development as a community although it did nothing to relieve the prevailing climate of seriousness. This was the arrival of the Finns. BC had the privilege of hosting many pioneer immigrants from Finland, and they were not always noted for taking part in mainstream community life, but the Gibsons Finns were different. These families, the Katos, the Wilanders, the Ruises, the Hintsas, the Lantas, the Sauris, the Nygrens and the Wirens, were refugees from a failed socialist Utopia called Sointula, founded in 1901 on Malcolm Island, 150 miles north up the Inside Passage. Having the agricultural bent of most Old Country folk, the Finns were drawn to the flat land on the bench behind the Gibsons waterfront. There they laboriously cleared most of the open fields which remained until lately as a prominent feature of the area known as Gibsons Heights. Driving through Gibsons Heights today you can tell the Finnish homesteads from the habit their founders had of placing buildings back in the middle of the property rather than at the edge nearest the road. A number of old farmhouses still stand well back from the highway in the midst of large fields.

As Socialist Utopians, these Finnish settlers had community building in the blood. They immediately set about organizing their new neighbours, erecting the first community hall, the first post office, a co-op store, and a co-op jam cannery for processing the berries which turned out to be the only thing that the poor glacial soils of Gibsons Heights produced on a commercial scale.

The Finns were veteran political campaigners and brought their radical leftist beliefs to bear on all community issues from education to medical care to religion. The WASP old guard were thoroughly scandalized by the rabble-rousing foreigners and mounted a heated defence of God and the King that made Gibsons a hotbed of political debate that still echoes down the corridors of time.

What is noteworthy is how successful the Finns were in bringing many of the other settlers around to their views. They found a staunch ally in the community doctor, Frederick Inglis, who in turn did his best to indoctrinate the local Methodist minister. The minister, who was struggling to square the pro-war position of the church with his own pacifist leanings, proved receptive enough to the radical talk to get himself fired by the local parish, whereupon he was forced to move his entire family into the doctor's house above the Gibsons wharf. In those close quarters the dialectic intensified, with the minister struggling to find a middle path between the firebrands up on the flats and the flag-waving mossbacks down on the Gibsons waterfront. The position he hammered out changed the course of Canadian history. The minister's name was James Shaver Woodsworth and he went on to found the most successful political party of the left in North America, a democratic-socialist hybrid of capitalism and socialism called the Co-operative Commonwealth Federation (CCF), later the New Democratic Party (NDP). In 1995, the majority of Canadians were represented by NDP governments, and Gibsons was only beginning to fade as a leftwing stronghold, as waves of well-heeled retirees fleeing the Lower Mainland finally began to swamp the old CCF spirit.

The house in which the founder of the CCF did his soul-searching still stands opposite Molly's Reach and surely deserves protection as one of the historic landmarks of Gibsons if not of Canada, but village authorities are no more inclined to let good things happen to it than to other heritage sites under their care.

It may be a bit of a romantic conceit nowadays with all the strip mall and condo development up the hill, but I have always felt Gibsons' centre of gravity is the part the city fathers tried to deep-six back in 1947, namely the landing. All BC coast communities, from Vancouver to Prince Rupert, are growing away from the working waterfronts that gave them their original reason for being, but Gibsons' small boat harbour remains busy and viable, supporting a handful of marinas, several shipyards, and one of the best government wharves left on the BC coast.

The red-railed government wharf, a sturdy, centrally located, well-maintained timber-and-piling dock provided by the federal Department of Transport (now the Coast Guard), has over the years been the most important public institution in every seafront village on the BC coast. In places without road access, the government wharf was where the steamers and larger freight vessels made their all-important landing on "boat day," as much a social as a working occasion, when all and sundry would gather on the foot-polished plank deck to visit, whether they had any boat business or not. The "guvermint worf" was the coast town's Piccadilly Circus and Times Square, where all the joyous arrivals and sad departures took place. Many government wharves have been downsized to eliminate their steamship-docking capacity, or eliminated by neoconservative political regimes anxious to disable all truly effective government services, but Gibsons remains one of the few that can still accommodate a sea-going ship as well as a ragtag population of old wooden tugs, ex-North Sea trawlers, evil-looking log salvage jet boats, rickety live-aboards, half-sunken hulks and other vessels of character, reputable and otherwise.

Boats are central to the lives of island people and near-island people. Aboriginal life on the Sunshine Coast was made possible by the existence of the ubiquitous cedar dugout, and the first wave of non-Indian pioneers such as the Roberts Creek Roberts paddled their possessions ashore in large clinker-built rowboats purchased in Vancouver from a transplanted Bluenose boatbuilder named Andy Linton. Settlement didn't kick into high gear until a regular steamer connection with Vancouver was established by the Union Steamship Company in 1888,

and ships of that company like the *Comox, Cowichan, Chelohsin* and *Capilano* play the kind of role in Sunshine Coast history that the Mardi Gras plays in the history of New Orleans, as in, "I met my first husband on the *Cowichan*, but then I lost him on the *Cynthia*."

When I cast backward for my first memory of the Sunshine Coast, what I come up with is a boat. A fifty-foot fish packer named the *Murpak I*, which my father had hired on May 24, 1950 to move my mother, me, my two sisters and our worldly belongings from Vancouver to our new logging camp home on Nelson Island. There is an undertone of unhappiness to the memory—of over-stressed parents barking orders unnecessarily harsh, of my baby sister greeting the strangeness with six hours of inconsolable howling, of my own deep insecurities about leaving the known world behind—but laid over this is the

Artist Jan Poynter's linocut interpretation of Gibsons' much-publicized working waterfront.

memory of adventure, the unexpected thrill of sailing off in the brave ship *Murpak I*.

Marking the years since are more memories of boats and trips on boats—the ex-rumrunner *Suez*, our leaky old camp tender that I piloted home through a foaming middle-of-the-night gale at age nine because the crew who invited me to come along on the weekly grocery run to Pender Harbour were too drunk to stand, let alone steer. The *Jervis Express*, an ex-World War Two Fairmile doing ungainly service as a passenger freighter, bringing our Christmas presents up from Vancouver two weeks late and soaking wet. The *Flash*, the backyard cabin cruiser my father built to fulfill his dream of owning the perfect boat, but which rotted on blocks without ever getting quite finished.

Fishing families in Pender Harbour mark off the periods of their lives not by births, deaths or natural catastrophes but according to the boats they owned at the time, as in, "It must have been before February 13, 1946 that Ma run off because that's when I got the *Okeefenokee Queen* and when she was here I still had the *Sea Bag*."

People even refer to each other by the names of their boats sometimes: "You're *Sea Aggressor*? I'm *Lonesome Polecat*. You corked me last August in Bear Bight!"

In modern times much of the boat life of the Sunshine Coast has been sacrificed to the Age of the Automobile, but road travel is still ultimately dependent on the ships of the BC Ferry Corporation, and no news will move up the seaweed telegraph faster than word the "Cow" (*Queen of Cowichan*) has ripped out the Langdale dock again, or the breakdown-prone "Crapilano" (*Queen of Capilano*) missed a sailing because of the Jervis Express (in this case the howling nor'wester that smokes down Jervis Inlet in January, named in memory of one of the boats least able to cope with it). People wouldn't consider getting married on the BC Ferries like they did on the "Union boats," but they remain an important social institution nonetheless. I sometimes feel I would lose touch with my neighbours completely if I didn't keep running into them on the ferry.

The boats at the government wharf in Gibsons are the boats of the coast's real boat people, and a visitor can learn more about the authentic maritime culture of the region in a half hour dock walk there than in weeks of haunting museums. With luck, she can also negotiate a good deal on some live-landed Howe Sound prawn or halibut from the hold of a longliner fresh in from Haida Gwaii. The Whiskey Slough float in Pender Harbour also shelters a handsome collection of commercial work boats, mostly flashy new gillnetters, and the government docks at Westview and Lund harbour smaller communities of working wharf rats, but not on the scale of Gibsons.

Some far-sighted early planner provided Gibsons with a waterfront esplanade that has recently been opened up to Sunday strollers, and this twenty-minute walk makes a great way to visit the Sunshine Coast's most famous stretch of beach. If you plan your hike from north to south you will come out just a crooked block from the Elphinstone Pioneer Museum at Gower Point and Gower Point, one of the better small-town museums you'll find.

Many visitors to the Sunshine Coast drive the entire hundred miles of the Sunshine Coast Highway never having really seen much actual sea coast and wondering why. One answer would be that nobody in a position to do so ever thought to make allowances for visitors who might want to get down to the water, or see more than the odd glimpse of it. But another answer is that there are some well-concealed points of access where one can slip off the highway and inhale a bit of seaweed-scented breeze if you know where to go. One of the nicest is out at the end of Gower Point Road where it turns into Ocean Beach Esplanade. Gower Point is itself one of the older settlements in the area, although it is quite distinct in character, having a long history as a summer cabin centre for vacationing Vancouverites. A lovely little provincial park, complete with a cairn commemorating Captain Vancouver's brief stopover in 1792, rests right at the water's edge by the mouth of Chaster Creek. The cobble beach is not for bare feet and the water is icy even in August, but there is no better place on the coast to barbecue a cob of corn and watch the sun explode in salmons and corals as it squelches its flames in the sea beyond Lasqueti.

ROBERTS CREEK

IF YOU FOLLOW GOWER POINT ROAD TO where it turns into Ocean Beach Esplanade and then follow Ocean Beach to where it dead-ends in the brush, you have gone as far north as you can and still be said to be in greater Gibsons. One further step and you enter into the domain of Roberts Creek. Roberts Creek is a diffuse, five-mile stretch of coast reaching from Gower Point to Wilson Creek. It is so formless geographically the casual visitor might make the mistake of thinking it is not really a community at all, merely surplus territory waiting to be used up by Gibsons and Sechelt sprawl.

Upon meeting any one of the 2,447 Creekers who occupy the territory any such impression would be quickly dispelled. There is no community on the Gulf with a more defiant sense of its own sovereignty. "The Creek" is a state of mind as much as a place, and the mind is as different from the serious, shift-working mind of Gibsons as the puckish spirit Harry Roberts is from the dour, sad ghost of George Gibson. Where Gibsons favours business-minded ex-bankers and storekeepers for mayor, the Creek's regional director all through the 1980s and '90s

Carving of whale marks the site of former steamer wharf at Roberts Creek, now a regional park.

was a bearded geography prof who lived in a solar house and built a bureaucratic barricade aimed at holding Sechelt and Gibsons sprawl at bay.

Roberts Creek is the Sunshine Coast's Haight-Ashbury, the place where the rebel consciousness of the 1960s found its most fertile ground and achieved its most extreme expression. Author Ken Drushka, who spent the summer of 1968 giving out government Opportunities For Youth grants to people who wanted to start communes, once told me he found as many eager applicants in Roberts Creek as in the whole rest of the province. But Creek elders like Doug and Helen Roy would say that the roots of back-to-the-land thinking go much deeper, and have lasted much longer as a consequence. In the book, *Remembering Roberts Creek*, Hubert Evans, who chucked the life of a downtown media celebrity for Creek existence back in 1927, remembered the incident that made up his mind, way back then:

In 1927 a couple seeking less-hurried lifestyles than they had found in cities visited Roberts Creek. During a stroll they stopped to watch an elderly man fastening wire claws to the end of a long cedar pole he had shaped. "For hooking up mussels, the big ones low down on the wharf piles," the man explained.

"Mussels for eating?"

"For catching shiners. Shiners make good cod bait. I aim to go cod fishing the day after." Three unhurried days to catch a cod! Then and there the couple knew their search had ended.

Hubert moved his family onto an acre of waterfront at the mouth of Stephens Creek and soon became an adept in the Creek lifestyle, writing assiduously until sales of his stories for children's magazines totalled $2,500 for the year. At that point he would purposefully down his pen and take the rest of the year off, cruising up and down the coast with his family in their 28-foot gasboat, the *Solheim*. When the latter-day wave of back-to-the-landers rolled around four decades later, Hubert was able to view them with some bemusement in his poem, "Flower Children":

> They came starry-eyed from the city
> to walk with nature
> But only to her chosen
> would she give her hand.

Evans' and Roberts' nonconformist, artistic, nature-loving spirits live on in the modern community, which includes the highest concentration of painters, musicians, potters, writers, homespun philosophers and ornery stumpranchers of any place on the coast.

The creek mouth, where Harry Roberts built the first store and community wharf, is still the nearest thing Roberts Creek has to a downtown, with a store, post office, school, several eateries, and just up the road a firehall, church, legion and a venerable old community hall. What it doesn't have any longer is a functioning wharf or any vestige of the busy harbour Harry Roberts developed back in the 1920s. Above the highway as well as below, the Creek's sloping south-facing sea exposure makes it a perfect theatre from which to contemplate the beauties of Georgia Strait, but modern Creekers are a landlubberly lot compared to their neighbours in Gibsons and Pender Harbour. Their geography leaves little choice. Among boaters, the shoreline from Gower Point north is known as "the Stretch," a harbourless gauntlet one must run between Gibsons and the shelter of the Trail Islands off Sechelt. Evans reflected on the ironies of Creekers' relationship to the sea in his poem, "Unrequited Love":

> "I love the sea," she tells me.
> Well and good, dear lady,
> but let me caution you
> the sea will not reciprocate.
> During my years here
> within sight of this house
> the following have drowned:
>
> 1 settler
> 4 towboat men
> 3 heedless boys
> 3 youthful canoeists
> 3 fishermen
> 1 toddler
> 1 bride-to-have-been

> As indicated by the foregoing
> the sea is not selective.
> It does not play favourites.
> Unlike Jehovah it has no chosen people.

As compensation for its pitiless lack of shelter, the Roberts Creek shore offers some of the coast's better beaches, though once again they're easy to miss from the highway. MacFarlane's Beach is a crescent of gravel and soft sand just downstream from the creek mouth which can be accessed from the old wharf right-of-way at the foot of Roberts Creek Road (now a regional park), and there is another rare patch of sand punctuated by massive wave-sculpted boulders at the tiny provincial park at the foot of Flume Road.

The Creek also boasts perhaps the most hospitable upland area on the Sunshine Coast, with thousands of acres of flattish land sloping gently back from the beach and on up the foot of Mount Elphinstone. Much of this land was cleared in the early part of the century by eager homesteaders who soon found the sad truth about the thin, acidic soil that underlays coniferous forests, and gave up farming for the more lucrative alternative of logging.

Poor as it is for food crops, the soil of the Sunshine Coast is one of the most outstanding timber growing sites on the planet and its original Douglas-fir forest was one of the wonders of the natural world. On the north end of the Sechelt Peninsula it gave rise to larger-scale railroad logging operations but some of the best timber on the lower end was destroyed in 1906 by a promethean forest fire which started in the area of the Boy Scout camp and thundered across the western face of Mount Elphinstone almost as far as Howe Sound. Miles of prime timber were reduced to skeletal snags and the ash in places was said to be ten feet deep. In dry winds it drifted like snow in a prairie blizzard.

The area eventually reseeded itself, with the result that today the lower slopes of Mount Elphinstone support one of the most densely-stocked second-growth fir forests in the province, almost ripe for reharvesting. This has not escaped the notice of the environment-conscious denizens of Roberts Creek, who have launched a spirited campaign to save the young forest from clear-cutting by the major forest companies. Instead they are urging it be preserved for selective logging by small tenure holders like Tom and Bill Wright, two local woodlot operators whose Witherby Tree Farm has been quietly proving for half a century that small can be beautiful in the BC woods.

It was the old overgrown stumpranches left behind by the early homesteaders-turned-loggers that were discovered by delighted commune-seekers in the 1960s. Crowe Road alone was once said to be the home of a dozen of these groups, and legend has it somewhere back in the bush one still endures. The jungles behind Roberts Creek are also reputed to conceal some 1960s refugees who, when all the hair fell out, were revealed to be scions of famous and wealthy families, and established comfortable estates with their inheritances. Yuppies hungering for the rural ambiance are squeezing out the last of the Creek's unreformed Age of Aquarius survivors, but the woods still harbour a few of the classic old tarpaper palaces strewn about with fabulous collections of junk. Perhaps there are still even a few marijuana-ranching operations. The drug trade was for some time Roberts Creek's most conspicuous economic activity, and until a few years ago it was not uncommon for local papers to carry accounts of drug-related beatings and shootings. Now it seems the business has either died down or established more traditional methods of credit management.

DRIVING NORTH ON THE HIGHWAY, IT'S NOT hard to tell where the influence of the Roberts Creek nature-lovers ends—at the point where the strip malls start back up again, just across the border between Roberts Creek District and Sechelt Municipality at Wilson Creek. Wilson Creek, Davis Bay and Selma Park form a generally unbroken continuum of subdivisions the rest of the way into Sechelt proper. The most notable feature is the stretch of oceanview motoring at Davis Bay where the highway fronts the shoreline of the bay. For many visitors this is the scenic highlight of their trip, the only good taste of open seascape they get on the much-touted scenic drive up the Sunshine Coast.

When you have spent your entire life in a place, certain locations come to have special meaning, and for me this is one. Forty years ago the gravel spit that juts out into Georgia Strait off Chapman Creek almost made me an orphan. Just before our family moved to the isolated camp in Green Bay that became our first Sunshine Coast home, my father was charged with the task of transferring the rickety camp tender *Suez* from Vancouver to Green Bay. All went well until he challenged the dreaded "Stretch," the exposed thirty-mile section of open gulf between Howe Sound and Sechelt. A big southeaster blew up and at the crucial moment, as Dad was straining to round the tide-whipped spit at Mission Point, the old

Chrysler Crown sputtered to a stop. He tried every trick in the book to restart it, but to no avail. There are not too many places on the shores of Georgia Strait where surf can be said to actually break, but Mission Point in a big southeaster is one. Dad fought as long as he could to keep the punky old rumrunner clear of the thundering surf with a pike pole, then he bailed over the side, planted himself firmly in the gravel of Mission Spit and personally held the heaving ten-ton vessel off the shore all night. In daylight he poled the derelict over to the Davis Bay wharf and staggered in to the then Selma Park Lodge. The suspicious manager was barely persuaded to admit him to a room where he convulsed with hypothermia for twenty-four hours, passing in and out of consciousness. Then he went down to the boat, cleaned the caked salt off all the ignition wires and proceeded to Green Bay where he found everyone wondering what had taken him so long. He often told me that night on Mission Point was a kind of turning point, where he started out a feisty young buck who thought he could face any physical challenge, but came away a sadder and wiser adult who realized he had limits. He also felt that in that one stormy night he had broken his health, which had been flawless until then but never after. My sympathy is tempered by the fact he was still doing the odd truck driving stint at age eighty-two.

I experienced my own brush with hypothermia at Davis Bay when I somehow got inveigled into trying my luck in the 1994 Polar Bear swim, forty-four years after Dad spent his night holding the *Suez* off the frigid winter waters of Mission Point. I managed the compulsory fifteen minutes, but was speechless with shock for the next six hours. They just don't make 'em like they used to.

Chilly as the water often is even in mid-summer, Davis Bay is still the most popular beach on the *Baja*, the site of a sometime sand castle contest that draws thousands and reduces through-traffic on the Sunshine Coast's main artery to a crawl all day. The old wharf is the last of the three steamer docks that used to offer relief to boaters navigating the Stretch, although nowadays it is only used by oil companies transferring fuel to the nearby tank farm. Site of the annual Charlie Brookman Fishing Derby for kids, the wharf has a faithful year-round clientele of sports fishermen, who catch a surprising number of good-sized cohos and springs on buzz bombs and other casting lures.

Above: The Gambier Island General Store. Though it was first settled a year before Gibsons Landing and once boasted an apple orchard with 1,000 trees, Gambier Island's year-round population remains tiny.

Right: Poet and novelist Peter Trower grew up in the old pulpmill community of Port Mellon and still lives and writes in nearby Gibsons.

Along green tunnels
sinewy alders spring up from the salmonberries
growth foams across old roads like gates closing
grouse rustle secretly
slugs move like severed yellow fingers
shrinking mudpools remember the last rain
sunshafts stab through the leaves...
time sings like a minstrel
in the harped forgotten forest...
I walk through witched green twilight
in suspicions of truth...
I am one below summer
burning in the neutral wood.
            Peter Trower, from "Along Green Tunnels"

City children bound for summer camp swarm the old steamship dock at Hopkins Landing, rarely used since the car ferry brought the Sunshine Coast into the age of the automobile in the 1950s.

History buff and patron of the arts, Gibsons native Sandy Gibb is a new-look logging operator who believes well-managed timber harvesting can continue indefinitely as a major economic factor on the Sunshine Coast. His Fleetwood Forest Products is the largest logging company based in the area.

Tranquil waters of Howe Sound mirror a perfect day on the Gibsons waterfront. Armours Beach in foreground.

Inner tube races at Armours Beach are always a highlight of the Gibsons Sea Cavalcade.

Its popularity with filmmakers has given Gibsons one of the most recognizable sea fronts in Canada.

Opposite: Well-known Canadian photographer Ken Bell, a Gibsons resident, never tires of documenting Howe Sound's changing moods. Here a rainbow forms over Keats Island.

The fondly remembered era before cars when everything depended on boats continues to prevail on Keats and Gambier islands, which are served by the passenger-only ferry Dogwood Princess.

Pre-war frame buildings like Molly's Reach, the Marine House, the Inglis House, Wynken, Blinken and Nod Apartments and Hill's Machine Shop, which has a marine ways in the basement, give the Gibsons sea front a historic character which attracts Sunday painters and moviemakers.

If this jet-boat and float shack look familiar, it might be because they were featured in the long-running Gibsons TV series "The Beachcombers." Since the program ended in 1989, props have returned to real-life beachcombing.

Above:
Gibsons from the air. Long the largest centre on the lower Sunshine Coast, Gibsons Landing was founded in 1886 and incorporated as a village in 1929. It became the Town of Gibsons in 1983. By the 1990s Gibsons and Gibsons Heights had a combined population of 6,000.

Right:
Abandoned fishboat hulk sags ignominiously on the beach as a January snowstorm blankets lower Gibsons.

The Gibsons Area

Gibsons pulls out all the stops for its annual Sea Cavalcade Parade.

Below: Fireworks light Gibsons Harbour at the climactic moment of the Sea Cavalcade, an annual summer fair in which Gibsons celebrates its maritime roots.

A stony headland known as "The Bluff" is one of Gibsons' most distinctive landmarks.

Snow falls so rarely on Lower Gibsons it is usually a cause for celebration.

Following pages: Once a small harbour busy with boats, log booms, sawmills, camps, stores and a landmark waterwheel, the mouth of Roberts Creek is now a quiet park.

Roberts Creek painter Maurice Spira is one of many professional artists who work from studios on the Sunshine Coast.

At his Roberts Creek foundry sculptor Jack Harman produces some of Canada's best-known bronze sculpture, including the 12' high equestrian monument of Queen Elizabeth on Parliament Hill.

The windswept shoreline fronting Roberts Creek is the area pioneer Charlotte Roberts originally dubbed "The Sunshine Belt," a term that caught on and grew until the whole area from Port Mellon to Desolation Sound became known as the Sunshine Coast.

Above: Gower Point, named by Captain George Vancouver when he overnighted there in 1792, is the location of a small but delightful park and one of the Sunshine Coast's prime sites for sunset-watching.

Old chapel on Beach Avenue is a quiet reminder of past times in Roberts Creek.

BEACH
CHAPEL
CAMPFIRE

Part Two

The Sechelt Area

Aerial view of Davis Bay area shows Chapman Creek estuary at Mission Point with the town of Sechelt in distance.

IF PRESENT-DAY ROBERTS Creek seems to carry on with the non-conforming, spiritual style of Harry Roberts, present-day Sechelt might be said to carry on in the mercantile, entrepreneurial manner of Herbert Whittaker. Whittaker was no more the founder of Sechelt than Roberts was of Roberts Creek, but he was just as much the guy who put it on the map. A mere stripling of eighteen when he arrived in Sechelt with his father Alfred in 1893, Whittaker was up to his elbows in land development within two years, subdividing the old Scales preemption into the original Sechelt townsite. Young Whittaker was a whirling dervish of commercial enterprise. By the time he was twenty-two he'd put up a twenty-one-room hotel, a store and a post office, and before he was done he would own two more hotels, a much larger store, a row of rental houses, a dance hall, a couple of sawmills, five logging camps, two commercial wharves and two steamship lines. Did I mention a farm? He also may have been the first full-time resident of the Sunshine Coast to own a motor vessel that existed solely to provide its owner with pleasure, a cabin cruiser called the *Resort*. He was the coast's first tycoon—and its first bankrupt tycoon. In 1924, following a period of illness, he lost his property to the bank, where the Union Steamship Company picked it up cheap and continued to promote Sechelt as a resort village.

Sechelt rivals Roberts Creek in its magnificent sweep of south-facing waterfront on Trail Bay, but since the old steamer wharf was dismantled in 1971, public use has pretty much been limited to enjoying the view. From a quarter-mile out, the sweeping crescent of white beach looks so inviting you wonder why it's not speckled with bathers, but closer inspection reveals egg-sized cobbles that make for more of a foot massage than most people want on their days off, and the three-knot current keeps the water temperature too bracing for comfort in anything but scorching weather. Still, the beachfront "Boulevard" which begins just west of the historic Sechelt Indian Reserve No. 2 on Wharf and runs west to Ocean Avenue, makes a rewarding five-minute walk, especially if you continue up to tiny but exquisite Snickett Park at the westward end, where the wave-polished granite ramparts do invite bare feet. From the 1920s until the 1950s,

this bumpy stretch of wagon path was white Sechelt's main street, giving access to two hotels, three general stores, a post office, a school, some houses and a row of rental cabins. Highlighted by the totem poles beside the first general store, it presented an impressive facade to anyone approaching the town by sea, which hundreds of picnickers did aboard Whittaker's steamers the *Tartar* and the *Sechelt*. The little town was regularly swamped with low-budget holidayers off work from Vancouver factories and offices, as Sam Dawe, skipper of the *Tartar*, remembered in *Helen Dawe's Sechelt*.

In those days before prohibition the hotel boasted a very fine bar with a view over the straits. Inasmuch as Mr. Whittaker at one time operated five logging camps and some shingle-bolting camps in or near Sechelt Inlet, at times it became somewhat rowdy...the attempt to mix tourism with loggers was not always too successful.

Two buildings from this era remained into the mid-1990s, clapboard bungalows with serpentine rooflines that were built by Whittaker in the 1920s. The last time I was in one of these houses, the one nicknamed *Kwicherkickin*, it was occupied by the writer Hajo Hadeler and the structure was so warped by time and uncertain foundations that whenever his little boy Jason let go of his toy truck it would go careening across the floor and fetch up against the wall on the low side of the room.

Sechelt's most striking physical feature is the narrow isthmus it occupies, which from the height of a passing floatplane seems barely sufficient to hold the outer waters of Georgia Strait apart from the 100 miles of landlocked shoreline of Sechelt, Narrows and Salmon inlets. Providing access between these two waterways has long been identified as one of the chief advantages of the site. Legend has it the Sechelt Indians were the first to try digging a canal through the sandy soil of the isthmus, which might have made sense in pre-smallpox times when the inner waters were more heavily settled than the outer ones. The canal brainwave has ebbed and flowed over the years, most recently in the 1980s when then-Mayor Bud Koch became noisily possessed of the notion, but the problem has always been that not that many people really need a $40-million canal in order to take small craft from the Gulf into Sechelt Inlet. Logging activity in the inlet has dwindled to a handful of stragglers, and apart from a very few holdovers from pioneer times like the legendary "Cougar Lady," a solitary trapper and woodsperson whose real name is Bergliot Solberg, there is virtually nobody living year-round beyond the Porpoise Bay–Tuwanek area. The brief day of fish farms, when some seventy operations appeared like an overnight plankton bloom in the early 1980s and as quickly washed away in a tide of bankruptcy, has passed. In the 1990s a different Sechelt mayor began touting the inlet as an "Inland Sea" packed with recreational wonders, but its appeal has always suffered in comparison with the more accessible cruising and better fishing on the outside. Still, for those who have already sampled the delights of Smuggler Cove, the Thormanbys, Pender Harbour, Hotham Sound and Jervis Inlet, Sechelt Inlet is a pleasant weekend cruising experience offering several pocket-sized marine parks, an unusual waterfall at Misery Creek that leaps out of a crack in the rock, and spectacular wilderness hiking into Phantom Lake. For those who like scuba diving on artificial reefs, there is also the scuttled destroyer HMCS *Chaudiere* at the mouth of Salmon Inlet.

In Bert Whittaker's day it must have seemed that the inlet was going to play a much bigger role in the town's future. It was alive with large railway logging camps, there was a brick factory at Storm Bay, there were fishing resorts up Salmon Inlet, and the settlements at Doriston and Clowhom must have seemed as likely to develop into permanent communities as Egmont or Pender Harbour. Whittaker cornered the up-inlet trade by building the first wharves on both sides of the Sechelt isthmus, and for three decades the wagon path that connected them was the busiest street in town. New opportunities opened up for men like "French Pete" Levesque, a party-loving roustabout who fell a big fir tree, hacked off two approximately round slices, attached them to a plank box, scrounged up a nag to pull it, and started the Peninsula's first overland freight hauling business. One day between deliveries French Pete retired to his shack and blew his brains out, an act only those of us who later tried to make a buck hauling on Sunshine Coast roads can fully appreciate.

It was not until the mid-1950s, when the Sunshine Coast Highway was completed with ferries at both ends, that the Sechelt's east-west axis along Cowrie Street began to overshadow north-south traffic along Wharf, but either way Sechelt was going to capitalize. Situated on a crossroads at the geographical centre of the *Baja* Sunshine Coast, Sechelt was and is the strategic location for a regional trading hub, and Whittaker's descendants have carried on with his example. It was a cousin of Whittaker's, E.S. Clayton, who grandfathered the family which still operates the ever-expanding Trail Bay Mall and several other leading businesses in town.

Black oystercatchers work busily at the edge of the tide in Davis Bay.

Despite its significant location, Sechelt has for most of its history played second fiddle to Gibsons in terms of size and influence, although the balance began to shift through the 1980s and '90s as more and more region-wide services followed the example of St. Mary's Hospital (formerly located in Pender Harbour) and set up shop in the middle of things. By the mid-1990s the two areas were about the same size, at roughly 6,000 people each. This trend is viewed with alarm by Gibsons, which is reluctant to relinquish its position as big sister among *Baja* towns and is loath to concede any advantages to its upcoast underlings for any cause. This leads to a standoff when it comes to such issues as pooling resources to build a recreation complex for the coast, which neither town can afford on its own but neither can bring itself to support unless the concrete gets poured within its own bailiwick. The result is a generally low level of services considering the combined tax base of the whole area, and duplication of what little there is. It has become quite popular for tub-thumpers of various stripes to decry the situation and call for a general union of all coastal communities from Egmont to Dogpatch, but until some Solomon solves the riddle of who will get the centralized infrastructure, the plan is likely to remain in the municipality of conjecture. For my part, I am just as happy. I believe our distinctive communities are a precious resource, and the longer the Sunshine Coast can avoid mushing together into one big faceless Surrey North, the better.

A certain noxious crank, reflecting on Sechelt's mercantile proclivities, once called it "a seaside shopping town that hasn't progressed an intellectual hair's breadth since Sinclair Lewis put the North American shopping town under glass in *Babbitt*." While it may be argued the Chamber of Commerce and Rotary Club play a more prominent role in Sechelt affairs than is perhaps advisable or safe, no town that calls its main drag Teredo Street can be all bad.

Indeed, modern Sechelt is a village of several dimensions. It boasts not one but two busy arts centres: Rockwood Lodge, a handsomely restored heritage building punctuating the western end of Cowrie Street, and the Sunshine Coast Arts Centre, located in an unusual high-tech log cabin on Trail Avenue. It has been for some years home of the Sechelt Festival of the Written Arts, an outstanding literary festival that has attracted the likes of Carol Shields, Alice Munro and Robertson Davies. Sechelt is also the home turf of the Sechelt Indian Band, one of the most progressive First Nations in Canada.

IF RECENT IMMIGRANTS TO THE SUNSHINE Coast have demonstrated a tendency to follow their own drummer, they appear to be continuing a trend well established by the area's first inhabitants. Before the arrival of European explorers in the late 1700s, the Sunshine Coast had been shared since the last ice age by three different tribes of native Indians, the Squamish (Howe Sound), the Sechelt (Sechelt Peninsula), and the Sliammon (Powell River). By all accounts they were exceptional peoples.

Although the Sunshine Coast tribes considered themselves unrelated, anthropologists group them together in a linguistic and cultural family known as Coast Salish. They enjoyed a comparatively comfortable existence owing to their benign climate and an abundance of easily obtained food, principally salmon, herring, venison and berries. The Coast Salish have never enjoyed the renown accorded by white Indian-fanciers to the Haida and Kwakiutl, probably because the Salish didn't erect forests of totem poles, didn't carve sea-going war canoes, and didn't produce world-class art—except on one notable occasion. On the other hand, they didn't use the bodies of freshly killed slaves for boat bumpers. What they did do was create a social order that came closer to that of modern democracies in terms of respect for human life and individual freedom. Among the Northern tribes, only those born to noble families could hope to achieve high standing through membership in secret cannibal and dog-eating societies, but every member of a Salish tribe had the opportunity to seek his or her individual *sulia* or power through a spirit quest that was open to all comers, and leadership was based on merit as much as on inherited privilege. There was no single, all-powerful chief, but a collective of male and female leaders all honoured with the same respectful term, in Sechelt *hiwus*.

One of the more imposing structures on the Sunshine Coast, the house of h=éwhiwus (House of Chiefs) is the administrative and cultural centre for the Sechelt Indian Band.

In their heyday, the Sechelt occupied the bulk of the territory now known as the Sunshine Coast with some eighty villages. So numerous were the lodge fires of the Sechelt nation, elders used to speak of a time when there was "one big smoke" from Gower Point to Saltery Bay.

Egg tempera painting by Sechelt artist Britton Francis reflects rugged beauty of Sechelt waterfront on Trail Bay.

The main tribal groupings were centred around four principal villages at Hunaechin (at the head of Jervis Inlet), Tsonai (at Deserted Bay, Jervis Inlet), Tuwanek (in Sechelt Inlet) and Kalpalin (Pender Harbour).

(Under the direction of Dr. Ronald Beaumont of the University of BC, the Sechelt have standardized Sechelt spellings using a specialized orthography, but because I don't have space to explain how the orthography works, I will eschew it for the more familiar of the anglicized usages and write "Sechelt" instead of "shíshálh.")

Unlike most other Coast Salish tribes, who stayed put in their ancestral villages year-round, the Sechelt congregated for the winter in one composite mega-village at Kalpalin on the shores of Pender Harbour. Although some band publications place their original population at 20,000, scientific estimates range between 5,000 and 8,000.

The undoing of this great Native nation began early on. The Roman Catholic missionary Father Leon Fouquet of the Oblate Order visited Kalpalin in 1860, urging all to abandon the beliefs of their ancestors and accept the god of the white man. Not surprisingly, Fouquet was sent packing. But only two years later, the Sechelt invited the Oblates back and submitted to a rigorous Christian regime under Father (later Bishop) Paul Durieu. Some writers present this simply as a case of children of darkness seeing the light, but there was more to it. Earlier in 1862 the worst smallpox epidemic in BC history swept like a tsunami through the coast's Indian communities. How many Sechelt died isn't known, but an unofficial head count several years later found them reduced to less than one-tenth of their peak numbers, and much of this decrease must have occurred in 1862. Clearly, the Sechelt people who turned back to the missionaries in the aftermath of the plague were not the same people who had so confidently rejected them two years earlier. With their own medicine men exposed as powerless against the menace of the white man's diseases, their leadership in shambles and the great family groups reduced to a few bewildered survivors, their appeal to the church was less a reasoned choice than an act of desperation.

It may also have been an act of fear. Major illness was understood by aboriginal peoples of the coast to be caused by hostile forces in the spirit world. The immediate source of trouble was typically thought to be a hostile medicine man, who would either have to be overcome or placated, depending on how powerful he was. When the early missionaries told native people the devastating epidemics were God's punishment for refusing His Word, it was all too plausible in terms of their traditional belief. The awesome force of the diseases suggested these new black-robed medicine men were too powerful to be resisted and had to be placated for the good of the tribe. It is no coincidence that the two greatest mass conversions in northwest coast history—by William Duncan among the Tsimshian and Durieu among the Sechelt—both occurred in the days immediately following the greatest smallpox epidemic in northwest coast history. With its terrifying example to back up his persuasions, Durieu was able to administer the sacrament of confirmation to every last man, woman and child in the Sechelt nation.

Like Duncan, Durieu followed the popular colonial

practice of removing converts from their ancestral grounds and gathering them together on a new site where the church could reign supreme. The site he selected was one Sechelt tribes had occupied only sporadically over the centuries because it was exposed to weather and attack, it lacked adequate drinking water and generally didn't have much to recommend it from an Indian point of view. This was Chatelech, the site of modern-day Sechelt. Over the next three decades the Oblates forged a Christian community at Sechelt which became the showpiece of "the Durieu System," a theocratic regime featuring police-state discipline and rigorous suppression of Native culture, later copied at Oblate missions among the Sliammon, Squamish, and others.

Durieu was a strict puritan who didn't allow his own French and Belgian priests to drink wine in private and in one oft-repeated anecdote broke up Sechelt preparations for a soccer tournament with the Nanaimos, confiscated the ball and ordered players and spectators alike to get to work ditching a swamp. In another story he prevailed upon some Sliammon men to paddle him down to Sechelt, a trip of some seventy miles. Midway they stopped for lunch. On previous occasions the arrangement had been that the priest would supply food for the men who gave their time to paddle him, but on this occasion Durieu was miffed because the band was resisting church pressure for increased cash contributions. He broke out a large basket and feasted himself ostentatiously before the hungry men. When one of them asked where their food was, Durieu said, "Eat wood, it is good enough for disobedient boys as you are." They had to carry the priest the rest of the way to Sechelt on empty stomachs. When Bishop E.M. Bunoz passed the same way fifteen years later, they were still talking about it.

Durieu espoused the belief that "Indians are only big children" and governed accordingly. The whole village was compelled to rise each morning at the first bell and attend church for prayers. An evening bell called them for a second daily round of prayers. Shortly after, a curfew bell was the signal for all lights to be put out. The punishment for missing church was the same as for adultery: forty lashes. On one occasion the flogging got so far out of hand one of Durieu's lieutenants, Father Chirouse, was convicted and jailed by civil court.

Native culture was strictly suppressed. As Bishop Bunoz wrote in a warm appreciation of his predecessor's system in 1941:

Our Indians had to give up all of their old fashioned amusements because they contained some traces of paganism and superstition. So they made bonfires with their century-old totem poles. They had to burn rattles, expensive coats and other paraphernalia of the medi-
cine men...Potlatches great and small were forbidden. Gambling, dancing and some winter festivities had to be abandoned. Bishop Durieu strictly exacted the abolition of the above practices because they were opposed to pure Christianity, but he knew well that the Indians had to have some amusements and that the pagan feasts had to be replaced by Christian ones.

Under Durieu's direction the Sechelt made a name for themselves by building a European-style townsite, touring a brass band and theatre troupe that staged elaborate passion plays around BC, and by diligently applying themselves to such nontraditional economic pursuits as logging, commercial fishing and commercial hunting for the fresh meat trade in Vancouver.

Viewing the results of Durieu's cultural makeover of the Sechelt three decades after it began, ethnologist Charles Hill-Tout reported:

Of all the native races of this province, they are probably the most modified by white influences. They are now, outwardly at least, a civilized people, and their lives compare favourably with the better class of peasants of Western Europe. Their permanent tribal home, or headquarters, contains about a hundred well-built cottages, many of them two-storied, and some of them having as many as six rooms. Each house has its own garden plot attached to it in which are grown European fruits and vegetables. In the centre of the whole stands an imposing church, which cost the tribe nearly $8,000 a few years ago. Nearby, they have a commodious and well-built meeting room, or public hall, capable of holding 500 persons or more, and a handsome pavilion or bandstand fronts the bay. They possess also a convenient and effective waterworks system of their own...every street has its hydrants at intervals of forty or fifty yards.

As a body, the Sechelt are, without doubt, the most industrious and prosperous of all the native peoples of this province...they owe their tribal and individual prosperity mainly, if not entirely, to the Fathers of the Oblate Mission.

IN FACT THE SECHELT HAD NOT FLOURISHED in the care of the church. Population had continued to decline at an alarming rate until by the time of the first official census in 1881, there were only 167 survivors left from the original body of over 5,000. The prim little community Hill-Tout viewed so approvingly in 1902 was but a sad remnant of the sprawling aboriginal nation that had united all the inlets and islands of the Sunshine Coast in "one smoke" a hundred years earlier. In the century since, the Sechelt have recovered steadily but slowly. By 1993 official band membership numbered

844, 400 of whom lived away from band lands. Most of the fabulous repertoire of songs and dances and ceremonial art which had enlivened the great festival season at Kalpalin was lost, but some were acquired by neighbouring tribes on Vancouver Island who still perform with them today.

One outstanding artifact remaining from prehistoric times is the "Sechelt Image," a twenty-inch-tall granite statuette discovered under a tree root by boys playing at Selma Park in 1921. I am informed that Sechelt elders of today view the figure as a mother holding her child *only*—with the emphasis on "only" because other observers, like the late anthropologist Wilson Duff, described it as "the very image of masculine strength, stated in the metaphor of sex. His head is powerfully masculine, and he clasps a huge phallus; the whole boulder, seen backwards and upside down, is phallic in form."

I stopped by the gallery just before writing this to check it over once more, and I'm afraid I have to side with Duff. For me, all doubt about the sexual connotations of the work is resolved by taking the posterior view, which slyly transforms the whole sculpture into a massive phallus, replete with bulging veins. Not to be overlooked is the anterior view, which reveals a prominent vulva.

Was some antique wit trying to sum up the entire sexual experience of humankind at one go? The way images of raging sexuality and serene parenthood are coupled in one ambiguous whole startles the viewer with its modernness, reaching across the erosion of the centuries with a cheeky freshness. No wonder Duff pronounced the Sechelt Image "a great work of stone sculpture" and the director of the Victoria Art Gallery, Richard Simmins, was inspired to make it the centrepiece of "Images: Stone: B.C.," a seminal exhibition of Northwest Coast Indian stone sculpture that toured Canada in 1975. A replica of this enigmatic, powerful masterwork, along with some good examples of Sechelt weaving and carving, can be viewed in the band's téms swíya Museum in Sechelt.

Today's Sechelt feel sadly cut off from the traditions of their aboriginal past, and they carry on few ceremonial activities compared to the neighboring Cowichan and Squamish. They pursue a vigorous language preservation project with the help of Dr. Beaumont and several families have revived the practice of giving potlatches (tl'e?enaks) to bestow traditional names, which they research in old church records. Elder Mary Craigan had tears in her eyes as she recounted to me her experience attending a Cowichan ceremony where she witnessed some of the ancient songs and dances which were once performed by her ancestors at Kalpalin. It was the first time she had heard them but they had worked a powerful spell over her she had no words to describe, as if pulling at something

deep inside. A traditional medicine man from outside has begun visiting the band, 130 years after shamanistic practices were banned by the Oblates. Granny Craigan struggles alongside other elders to excavate memories of their people's past to fulfill younger members' reawakening thirst for tribal identity, but it is hard digging. Indian or non, who could say what their ancestors did and thought over a century ago, especially when the main written record has been kept by people dedicated to erasing the heritage?

Something that has survived intact is the Sechelt's talent for commerce. They have been involved in the operation of an offshore trawler, a local airline, a salmon hatchery, an office and cultural complex, a large gravel-mining project, a McDonald's restaurant franchise and other business enterprises.

The Sechelt Image, a stone sculpture considered one of the masterworks of Northwest Coast aboriginal art, was discovered by children playing in Selma Park. Controversy rages as to whether it is a simple madonna or something more.

But it is in the political arena that the Sechelt have most distinguished themselves. From the earliest times when Chief Tom Tsohnye made land claims representations to Victoria, through the activism of such leaders as Caspar John, Joe La Dally, Dan Paull, Reg Paull, Charlie Craigan, Henry Paull, Stan Dixon, and Clarence Joe—a consummate statesman who addressed both the Canadian House of Commons and the United Nations—the Sechelt charted their own course through Canadian politics, far in advance of most other First Nations groups.

Their first goal was to free themselves from the shackles of the Canadian Indian Act, which deprived them of the full rights of citizenship and greatly restricted their mercantile inclinations. After a long campaign by a succession of Sechelt leaders, the federal parliament passed Bill C-93, The Sechelt Indian Band Self-Government Act of 1986, making them the first band in Canada to achieve native self-government. This proved controversial within the community of First Nations, since the Sechelt had taken a very pragmatic view of self-government, one characterized by the Grand Council of Crees as "identical to the model of the municipalities." This is not quite true since the Sechelt have extra-municipal powers over education, social services, health and public order, and section 38 of the Self-Government Act declares that the "constitution of the Band or the law of the Band" can take precedence over the laws of BC. Other bands held out for something closer to full provincial status and denounced the Sechelt solution as a sellout. The Sechelt view the grander claims as unrealizable, and hold that gains negotiated under their self-government agreements are underestimated by their critics.

Since 1986 more bands across Canada have been taking a second look at the Sechelt model, and the Nishga'a settlement of 1996 owes something to it, but for the most part the Sechelt remain defiantly out of step with their brethren on the national stage. For the original oddball residents of the Sunshine Coast, that is perhaps just as it should be.

AN EXCELLENT WAY TO PAUSE AND REFLECT upon one's visit to Sechelt is by taking an ale and chowder on the sundeck of the Wakefield Inn, a comforting old log lodge overlooking the beach at Wakefield Creek in West Sechelt. "The Wakefield" was built as a private mansion for a depression-era policeman named T.D. Sutherland, a multi-talented operator who acted as game warden and bossed the local relief gangs, among other things—more things than sometimes served the true course of justice, according to Hubert Evans. Sutherland was paid by the head for the destitute workers under his charge and Hubert used to bedevil him by luring men away from the relief camps and showing them how to make an independent living handlining salmon from rowboats.

There are no longer any handliners to be seen from the Wakefield's panoramic view, but wildfowl can often be seen—and heard—transacting noisy business down at the creek estuary. If you have your birding glasses you may be able to pick out humungous sea lions sunning themselves on the reef between Trail Island No. 2 and Trail Island No. 3. My father also instructed me on an infallible method of reading weather signs from this charmed location, which I am now prepared to reveal publicly for the first time. If wind is coming, you will see a whole pile of tugboats with log booms all clustered in behind the Trail Islands. This is the last shelter before the Stretch and the tugs won't pass by unless they've heard on their radios there's enough calm weather for them to run the gauntlet down into Howe Sound or the Fraser River. So if you see tugs with booms parading by, it means at least six hours before any serious wind.

Chapman Creek provides domestic water supply to most of the lower Sunshine Coast.

Indeed, an afternoon at one of the Wakefield's view tables may reveal many of nature's wonders. Inside the pub itself you may be lucky enough to spot authentic examples of the local working class peasantry, easily distinguishable by their traditional Sunshine Coast dress— battered baseball caps, red suspenders, grey Stanfield underwear tops serving as outerwear—a fashion known locally as the "Texada tuxedo"—and elastic-sided boots known as "fishermen's slippers." You can also detect true locals by their placement in the pub—away from the windows with their back to the view. This isn't to say their talk is any less concerned with solving the mysteries of the universe. It's just that they've got the view memorized.

Scoundrel or not, Sergeant Sutherland's architectural taste is not to be faulted. On a warm summer afternoon his old ill-got mansion can be hard to pull yourself away from, as many a weaving motorist has discovered. There are rooms at the Inn but they may be the only ones in Christendom the management itself advises you not to rent. I have never wanted to test their opinion in the matter.

JUST NORTH OF WAKEFIELD—THE HIGHWAY IS actually running west at this stage, but locals think of it as north—the route up the Peninsula divides between the new highway and the old highway, now called Redrooffs Road. Redrooffs Road snakes along the waterfront for about five miles to the tiny village of Halfmoon Bay and doesn't actually provide many open views, but it does let on to some fine places to get down to the sea. The first of these is at Sargeant Bay, where the Regional District has recently created a small park featuring a wildfowl marsh and a very pretty pebble beach. Another worthwhile stop comes up a few miles farther along, where a steep lane lets down to Welcome Beach. The name has an ironic tinge, for while the antique summer cabins that crowd the seafront esplanade are picturesque and the beach itself is very welcoming, the inhabitants of this cozy corner of paradise have a way of making non-residents feel as welcome as skunks at a garden party. You can reassure yourself that nobody owns the beach and brazen out the stares, or retreat to the regional park a few minutes' drive up the road at Cooper's Green. This also has a gravel wading beach along the eastern shore of Halfmoon Bay, and makes a good base for one of the most remarkable days of micro-cruising or gunkholing it is possible to take.

The Halfmoon Bay–Secret Cove area is probably the nearest thing to a saltwater labyrinth one is likely to find this side of Homer's Aegean. The sea-flooded stone formations here are as intricate as the folds of Einstein's brain, and the average brain can become thoroughly befuddled trying to keep track of which filament-like passageway, which hidden lagoon or which miniature islet is which.

Smuggler Cove Marine Park is the most famous example of this "drowned landscape," but Frenchman's Cove on the west shore of Halfmoon Bay is equally fine. Secret Cove just up the shore offers more of the same on a somewhat coarser scale, heavily overlaid with condos and marinas, including one quite decent ocean-view bar and restaurant at Jolly Roger Inn—although Lord Jim's Lodge just up the shore at Ole's Cove keeps more predictable hours. The area truly offers one of the most mesmerizing boating experiences on the coast, but it is all in miniature. A sea kayak would be a good vehicle for exploring it, and Cooper's Green offers good launching for car toppers or runabouts. The smaller the boat the more of the area's impossible intricacy you can probe.

Across Welcome Pass, joining North and South Thormanby islands is Buccaneer Bay, a low sandy spit with the sweetest swimming and sunning beach south of Savary Island. South Thormanby was preempted at the turn of the century by a sober British ironmonger named Calvert Simson, who at the time was storekeeper of the Hastings Mill Store in the town of Granville before it became Vancouver. He built a summer home beside the spit, cleared a farm down at the south end and lavished the island with fussy care for half a century before turning it over to his son George Joe, who carried on in the same manner until 1975, when he persuaded a reluctant provincial government to accept it as a free gift to the people of BC. Simson Marine Park is larger than Vancouver's Stanley Park or New York's Central Park, and after paddling through the seal rookery at Bertha Rock, poking your nose into the enchanted granite grottos on the south end and picnicking at the old farm, you will probably agree it's more attractive than either. It's sobering to think we almost didn't get it because the conservative politicians of the day didn't want to forgo a few dollars' worth of private land taxes.

Provided the log tugs are still indicating fair weather, a good way to top off the day's paddling is to pay a visit to the Sunshine Coast's only lighthouse, on Merry Island just a cattywampus across the chuck from Simson Park. As late as 1996 it was still a manned station, but federal bureaucrats in faraway Ottawa were waging a relentless campaign to replace the keepers with automated gadgetry that would ultimately be more expensive to maintain, would not provide the tugs with weather reports they could trust, and would not dash out to save you should your kayak be surprised by a westerly squall. It's the kind of thing that keeps debate on the merits of confederation a live issue on the West Coast.

Cougars are frequently sighted in Sunshine Coast backyards. This fine specimen is depicted by Gibsons artist Liz Mitten-Ryan, one of BC's most popular wildlife painters.

The fine natural sand, panoramic view and good skimboarding conditions at Mission Point give Davis Bay one of the most happening beach scenes on the lower coast.

Right: Glacial Phantom Lake, a challenging hike inland from the head of Salmon Inlet, is one of the coast's scenic jewels.

Porpoise Bay Park near Sechelt offers warm summer swimming and beautiful views of Sechlet Inlet.

A kildeer casts its reflection in the smooth sands of Davis Bay.

Following pages: Views over the old steamer wharf at Davis Bay are sometimes so spectacular busy ferry traffic slows to a crawl to admire it.

Detail of totem pole on Sechelt band lands.

First Nations participants ready themselves to paddle across Georgia Strait in the Save the Strait Marathon, mounted annually to publicize the Strait's environmental problems.

The Raven's Cry Theatre, located in the Sechelt Indian Band's headquarters complex, provides a focus for cultural activities by First Nations and non-First Nations groups.

Only sporadically occupied in pre-contact times, the Trail Bay site known as Chateleech became the home village of Sechelt Nation when Father Durieu established his mission there and renamed it Sechelt in the 1860s.

Sechelt elder Gilbert Joe spins his magic before an audience at the annual Rockwood Storytelling Festival.

Sechelt elder Theresa Jeffries became the first Sechelt Band member to graduate from the BC public school system in 1950, went on to a successful professional career and served as a band councillor.

Rockwood Lodge, built in 1936, has been carefully preserved as a centre for community activities and is Sechelt's most prominent heritage building.

Stormy fall skies gather over the government wharf at Porpoise Bay, Sechelt's main doorway to Sechelt Inlet.

The Solberg sisters, Bergliot and Minnie, grew up in the bush around Sechelt Inlet, sometimes working as loggers, and continued to follow an independent life as trappers and hunters into their seventies. Here Bergie, dubbed "The Cougar Lady" in the local press, appraises a freshly-stretched hide at her Sechelt Inlet rancherie, as Minnie looks on. Both agree the hardest thing about their lives in the wilds is increasing amounts of official red tape they must contend with.

Nonchalant gull seems completely unperturbed by massive sea lions.

The Sechelt Area

Right: Tetrahedron peak, a landmark visible for miles on the Sunshine Coast.

Below: Sun sets over mountain tarn on the Tetrahedron. Area was reserved for park use after a heated debate between loggers and conservationists.

Opposite: The Caren Range contains trees over 1,500 years old, among the most ancient in Canada. These first-growth cedars date back before arrival of white man on coast.

Far right: Blacktail deer are numerous on the Sunshine Coast.

Welcome Passage between Thormanby Islands and mainland shore is frequently busy with marine traffic.

Opposite: Looking down Welcome Passage at Merry Island Lightstation, up until 1996 the only manned lighthouse on the Sunshine Coast.

The full extent of Smuggler Cove's labyrinthine complexity can only seen from above.

Below: Inimitable setting makes Smuggler Cove irresistible to small boaters.

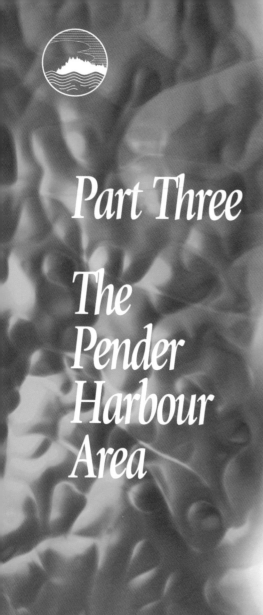

Part Three

The Pender Harbour Area

Restored classic vessel *Argonaut II* revisits its glory days as a missionary launch during bi-annual Mission Boat Reunion Days in Pender Harbour. The unique semi-annual event is sponsored by the Sundowner Inn, formerly a Columbia Coast Mission hospital, and celebrates the coast's maritime history.

Pender Harbour duplicates the drowned landscape complexity of the coves on a yet larger scale. The main harbour is only a mile and a half in length, but taking all the wrinkles into account, it has 103 miles of total shoreline. The whole performance involves three coves, six lagoons, twenty bays, twenty-nine reefs, thirty-one islands, one tidal narrows, one drying pass, two reversing saltwater waterfalls and Whiskey Slough. It takes ninety seconds to go from Pope Landing to Irvines Landing on the other side of the harbour in a slow kicker boat, or half an hour to drive by fast car, which is why for the first half-century Pender people did everything by boat—shop, visit, go to school, go to church. With dozens of little kickers crisscrossing the lagoons and bays at all times of the day and night, and a dock in front of every home, the comparison to Venice was obvious, but nowadays most people find it somehow more convenient to make the half-hour drive. The community is still laid out around the harbour, however, and it is only when toured by water it really makes sense. Negotiating the twists and turns by auto, it can take years before new residents can honestly say they know just where they are at any given time, and few long-term Harbourites could draw the place accurately without checking a map.

Such crenellated geography has worked its influence on the nature of the community. In Indian times the villages were separated from each other, as if compartmentalized by the landscape. People in the main village of Sawquamain in Garden Bay had limited contact with those at the Sallahlus village in Madeira Park, whom they considered without status. Present-day Garden Bay residents have at times been suspected of feeling the same way about Madeira Parkers, and vice versa. When I first came to the Harbour in 1950, its small population was partitioned into resolutely separate communities at Irvines Landing, Pope Landing, Donley Landing, Garden Bay, Kleindale and Madeira Park. Each place had its own school, store and community hall and tried to have as little as possible to do with the others. Turf wars over such matters as where to locate a new high school or credit union office were savage. Life was complicated further by a social structure based on big families, each firmly rooted in its own territory. The Lees held sway at Irvines, the Reids in Garden Bay, the Kleins at Kleindale, the Warnocks in Bargain Harbour, the Camerons and MacKays in Whiskey Slough. Before the Second World War, when they were interned on two hours' notice, there had been another quite separate group made up of Japanese families—the Ikedas,

Aerial view of Pender Harbour. Harbour was charted by British hydrographer G. H. Richards, who named it for his colleague Daniel Pender in 1860. Settled from 1900 onward as a fishing and logging community, its fabulous jumble of islands, bays and lagoons attracts increasing numbers of vacationers and retirees. 1996 population of 2,500 is only half what it was when Sechelt Nation wintered here prior to 1862.

Kawasakis and Okasas. When the Anglican minister Rev. Alan Greene of the Columbia Coast Mission began trying to organize Harbourites to construct the central Sunshine Coast hospital at Garden Bay in the late 1920s, he had the damndest time trying to get people to put aside their native animosities, and his daughter Barbara told me he was bedevilled by the community's irascible nature all the years he ran the hospital.

The poet Patrick Lane, a sometime Middle Point resident who moved back to the coast in the 1990s after living fifteen years on the prairies, remarked that the people of the coast in general were strikingly in-turned compared to the prairie types, who are much more open and sociable. The difference was so marked and so general he couldn't help thinking the wide-open geography of the prairie and the closed, compartmentalized geography of the coast were somehow reflected in the personalities of the people. In this sense Pender Harbour is like the coast in general, just a little moreso.

IT'S HARD TO CONTEMPLATE THE CENTURY OF non-Indian history of Pender Harbour without being aware how insignificant it is beside the Indian history of the place. Although it is well established that the Harbour was the winter home of the Sechelt Nation and one of the larger Indian communities on the West Coast, very little has been written on it and no serious study has been made of the area's very rich archaeological history. The anthropologist Homer Barnett, who visited Pender Harbour in 1935, mentions only the main settlement at Sawquamain in Garden Bay and one other to the south—presumably Sallahlus at Bargain Narrows. My own experience from a lifetime of excavating around Pender Harbour—not as an archaeologist, but as an interested ditch digger—is that there must have been almost continuous settlement around the entire 103 miles of harbour shoreline. I once had a job installing a sewer system on the Sallahlus reserve and found myself digging down in ancient fire ash and clamshell deposits to a depth of six feet, encountering not a few human skulls along the way. There was another large deposit of bone-laden midden soil at Irvines Landing at the mouth of the Harbour, and sizable ones at Gerrans Bay and on the fertile mudflats at the head of Oyster Bay, a site known as Smeshalin. When my father and I were excavating basements around Pender Harbour in the 1960s I became accustomed to rooting up cooking rocks and clamshell anywhere there was a pocket of dirt big enough to sink a muckstick into. Many sites were chock-full of human remains, sad evidence of the fate that befell these historic villages.

The Sechelt traditionally left their dead above ground on special burial islands like the two unnamed islets at the north end of Bargain Narrows. My school mate Ab Haddock and I lived on opposite sides of Gerrans Bay a stone's throw from those islets, and he used to make me jealous with all the nifty artifacts he dug up on them, but the rest of us kids lacked the nerve to disturb them. We were afraid of awakening smoldering embers of the last smallpox epidemic, which to us seemed still to lurk very near at hand, although it had died out a century earlier. It was easy to see that such a tiny burial ground would have been inadequate during the great plague of 1862, when the people fell in such numbers survivors were forced to convert many of the prime village sites into mass graves. More burying took place after the Sechelt's conversion to Catholicism, when the priests ordered that remains which had been set out in the traditional way be gathered up and placed underground in the European manner. There were dozens of bone-filled midden sites around the shores of Pender Harbour, many of them sizable, and most uncatalogued. Since it takes many years to build up an inch of permanent midden soil, these heavy deposits bear witness to the immense scale and intensity of the living that must have taken place here before the Europeans arrived with their deadly diseases. It's enough to make Gilbert Joe's estimate of 20,000 residents seem plausible, but even if the lowest estimate of 5,000 is correct, it would have made Kalpalin more densely populated in 1800 than Pender Harbour was in 1996—and that was just counting local residents. During big feasts, potlatches, or trading days, that number would be swelled by other Salish groups visiting from neighboring areas.

Viewing the modest all-white village of 2,500 reposing on the shores of the landlocked harbour basin today, it's hard to picture the same scene rocking under the sway of ten or twenty thousand celebrants, but if you'd dropped in between October and March a few brief centuries ago, that may well be what you'd have seen.

The Salish had an admirable grasp of what really mattered in life. They were tremendous workers and they laboured mightily all summer putting up dried salmon and making salal berry leather as well as dozens of other labour-intensive tasks involved in maintaining well-run stone-age households, like weaving watertight baskets of spruce root and washing used ones with a putrefied fungus known as *xwat'Kimunach* or "thunder shit." Everyday dress consisted of aprons made of deer hide or woven from cedar bark. Cedar bark was also woven into blankets and robes, as was wool from mountain goat and special long-haired dogs. Twine for fishing line and nets was woven from nettle fibre. Plentiful stands of red cedar provided easily worked building materials for dugout canoes, feast bowls and plank-walled dwellings, some of which were enormous. According to pioneer ethnologist Charles Hill-Tout, who studied the Sechelt in the summer of 1902, Sechelt houses had "a platform about two feet high and

Artist Gaye Hammond's conception of Sawquamain, winter headquarters of the 5,000-strong Sechelt Nation at Garden Bay in Pender Harbour prior to 1862. Coast Salish longhouses were enormous, Simon Fraser having measured one 800 feet long near Chilliwack.

five or six feet broad erected all around the inside walls. This served as seats or lounges for the occupants during the day, and during the night as beds. Some ten or twelve feet above this platform small isolated cubicles or sleeping rooms were constructed...Each family partitioned off its allotment from the rest by means of hanging mats."

The work of the Salish summer was performed with the aim of freeing the winter for social activities. Anthropologists are fond of referring to the winter activities of the Salish as "ceremonials" which they depict as some kind of joyless neolithic ritual. My old Squamish friend Dominick Charlie, who kept performing his sensational

when he approached a beach where people were dancing around a campfire, but turned into killer whales and swam away when he got close. In the dream that followed he got not only the dance and a song, but the killer whale's power to hunt seals, sea lions and porpoises. Another prominent man had the wolf dance, which he got when he fell and wounded his leg while stripping bark from a tree. When he awoke a wolf was licking his wound. In his dream he received a song featuring the cry of the wolf and a dance in which he ate the flesh of live dogs. Men's dances tended to be associated with major animals like the bear and mountain goat, while women were often left with lesser spirits like the duck, crane, quail and even the blowfly.

In addition to dancing, there were events of more distinctly spiritual nature such as initiation rites for young dancers taking possession of their own special dances and performances by medicine men. Sechelt shamans were particularly noted for their miraculous performances. The Tsonai leader Joe La Dally told anthropologist Homer Barnett of an occasion when a shaman named Kaltopa was called to attend a dying man. He brought with him the skins of seven different animals—otter, mink, raccoon, fox, loon, eagle and marten. After singing his spirit song, he blew on each skin and it came to life, scampering around on the floor uttering its natural cry. He then covered his head with a blanket and began to grope on the floor in search of the patient's missing soul. His own spirit was thought to have departed from his body at this point because at length he uttered a *whoo-ing* noise as if returning from a great distance. Finally the shaman rose, holding the retrieved soul in his hands. When it was returned to its rightful place the patient showed immediate signs of recovery, and his brother asked the shaman if he knew who'd taken the errant soul. The shaman said that he indeed did, whereupon the brother requested the evil-doer be put to death. The shaman again covered his head and began groping on the floor. After about half an hour the sounds of the returning spirit were heard once more, and the shaman leapt to his feet to reveal in the palm of his hand a tiny human body. He held the miniature form over the fire and squeezed it until blood ran out between his fingers, then dropped the small shape into the flames. At that moment a well-known Comox shaman keeled over stone dead, according to a Sechelt villager who had been visiting in Comox.

His duties completed, Kaltopa deflated his skins, packed up and left. The purpose of the skins had been to watch over the patient while the medicine man was out of his body stalking his foe in the spirit realm.

Barnett was able to obtain a corroborating version of this story from another Sechelt elder, Charlie Roberts, who added that Kaltopa's return was assisted by other

leaping deer dance until he was in his eighties, remembered it differently. "In them old times," Dominick told me, "we just dance and dance all winter long. Just dance and dance. Everybody he go to that big house and dance all night long and all day long. All winter he keep doing that. Oh, we had great times in them old times."

Great times. That's what the Salish winter was all about. Most people had their own special dance which had come to them in a dream or vision accompanied by a song, and often gave them a special power associated with an animal. One renowned hunter imitated killer whales in his dance. He had got this dance one night

Sechelt shamans who guided him back with choruses of their own *whoo-ing* in answer to his. Roberts added that he'd seen another shaman who could perform the miracle of bringing animal skins to life, and in addition possessed a big quartz crystal he could activate to dance and whirl around on the floor with a whining sound. Shamanic performances of this kind were a regular and popular feature of winter dances, along with feasting and potlatching, the ceremonial giving of property to enhance status. There were also lively trading extravaganzas, especially among the Sechelt, who have always been among the coast's great wheeler-dealers.

Kalpalin's principal settlement at Sawquamain, in the area now known as Garden Bay, was crowded with seven huge longhouses, four ranked one behind the other while the other three ran crosswise farther inland. Each had an attached woodshed and a spacious outdoor platform suitable for staging potlatches, an architectural feature my friend Gilbert Joe refers to as "the Sunshine Coast's first sundecks." Like modern-day homes on the Sunshine Coast which announce themselves to passing traffic as "Taki-Teasy" or "Dunworkin" (my favourite is "Sechelter"), each of the Sawquamain lodges had its own name. There was "Right on the Beach," "Back Side House," and "Down in the Hole." The largest house Lester Peterson records as "The Kluh-uhn'-ahk-ahwt," (tl'e'le-nakawt, or potlatch house), used only when the far-flung villagers were gathered together for communal events. There were no totem poles but "Right on the Beach" had a sea lion head carved onto the end of the ridgepole and lodge 5 had posts topped with carvings of eagles. Salish houses weren't as finely crafted as those of the northern tribes, but they were bigger. Simon Fraser observed one near Chilliwack which was 800 feet long and 300 feet wide, and Charlie Roberts told Hill-Tout the greatest of the lodges at Sawquamain towered fifty feet in height.

NOT ALL OF THE SECHELT'S TROUBLES BEGAN with the arrival of the white man, of course. The main problem was their vulnerability to attack by other Indian tribes, a vulnerability increased by their wealth and their nonviolent nature. The word "sch'ek'lt" or "fort" occurs frequently in Sechelt place names, and according to Peterson a real fort replete with wooden palisade and moat stood near the head of Jervis Inlet until historic times. Another fort existed on Thormanby Island, where the exposed Sxwelap village made frequent use of it to fend off sea-going marauders from Kwakiutl territory. My old school chum Ron Remmem, whose family home in

Pender Harbour was close to the Sechelt's long-vanished winter capital of Sawquamain, used to talk about finding what looked like an ancient fort site on the slopes of nearby Mount Daniel. This matches stories Peterson collected of a fort on Mount Daniel which was used to shelter women and children during raids on Sawquamain. Barnett reports the big houses of Sawquamain had "subterranean retreats ready for use in case of surprise attacks...entered by tunnels leading from hidden openings inside." Clarence Joe used to tell me his people also kept sentries posted on Mount Daniel—and at many other places including Cape Cockburn to the north and Spyglass Hill to the south—to provide early warning of any suspicious traffic in surrounding waters.

"Moon Rings," circles of stones placed atop Mount Daniel by Sechelt maidens during their puberty rituals.

Most raids were small affairs done by piratical rovers who picked off small groups of women and elders left unprotected during fishing or hunting forays, but large-scale massacres were not unknown. Peterson mentions a grassy flat east of Cockburn Bay on Nelson Island which got its name, *Swalth*, "from the fact that much blood was spilt there." He also used to tell me that the rocky knoll next to the property I grew up on at Madeira Park "was forever cursed by a powerful medicine man because of the slaughter suffered there by his people at the hands of early nineteenth-century raiders."

BY THE TIME I FIRST SAW PENDER HARBOUR IN 1950, only a few traces remained of the teeming, robust Salish city that made the Sechelt one of the great powers in the Northwest Coast Indian world. At Sakinaw Bay you could still trace among the barnacled beach rocks vague outlines of the elaborate stone fish trap that Professor Hill-Tout had described as a masterpiece of stone-age engineering a half-century earlier. Not long after, loggers perched an A-frame on the nearby bluff to skid logs out of

Sakinaw Lake and promptly obliterated all trace of the ancient wonder. Atop Mount Daniel you could still trace outlines of the stone circles which were placed by girls during puberty rituals. In 1950 the aged chief Dan Johnson and his wife lived in a tumbledown shack that was all that remained of Sawquamain with its seven enormous longhouses. Eugene Paul lived on a landlocked scrap of land in Gerrans Bay and the Julius family lived near the mouth of the Harbour on a barren group of islets locals referred to as the "Indian Islands." The white folks had taken everything else, leaving the Sechelt band as a whole with only four acres of reserve land for each of their drastically reduced numbers, in contrast to the eighty acres per capita provided Native peoples elsewhere in Canada—a gross inequity which caused the Sechelt to start one of the first Native land claims actions, back in the 1880s. In the 1990s they were still taking out full-page ads in Vancouver newspapers and threatening utility closures in attempts to get government action on their grievances.

WHITE SETTLEMENT IN THE HARBOUR WAS shaped by the same factors that shaped the formerly great Indian community—the excellence of the shelter and the abundance of local fisheries, especially herring. Pender Harbour's herring stocks are fished out now, but they were a natural wonder once. In the words of pioneer Martha Warnock, the place "was polluted with herring, you'd kill a thousand just rowing to the store, clobbering 'em with the oars, you couldn't help it." During my childhood in the 1950s, after two generations of mechanized onslaught by the fishing industry, herring were still so plentiful people used them for pig feed and fertilizer. Jigging a bucket of herring using many-hooked lines or "jigs" baited with embroidery thread, was an afternoon ritual on late summer days, and only took a few minutes. You would never bother winding the line in if it only had one or two fish tugging on it; you'd wait until there were eight or ten jerking away and it was too heavy to jig. Then you'd take them home and try to talk Gran into making "soused." As my school chum Ted Lee remembers the recipe, the herring were split from the dorsal side and the backbone removed, then covered with black pepper and rolled from the head end. Then they were placed in a baking pan filled with diluted vinegar and baked at a low heat until the bones were soft. Soused herring. It's right up there with wild blackberry pie.

In Native times herring were scooped up using a contraption called a herring rake, which consisted of a long stick bristling with bone needles. In late August just as afternoon was sliding into evening, you could fill a small dugout to the gunwales in a matter of minutes by sweeping the rake through the harbour water in the manner of an oar. What was particularly convenient about

herring from the Sechelt point of view was that they spawned in the middle of the winter when clams and dried salmon were starting to get over-familiar. You'd wake up one morning in late February or early March and the harbour shoreline would be plastered for miles with a translucent blanket of sticky, inch-thick roe. If you'd been on your toes you would have hung a bunch cedar boughs in the water overnight, and they'd be puffed up with roe just as if somebody'd come along and sprayed them with urethane foam. Still today, if you were to show up on the Sechelt band lands with a suitcase full of smoked herring roe on cedar boughs, you could have just about anything you cared to name, short of the McDonald's franchise.

There is a shadowy legend that the first non-Indian to occupy the Harbour was a Chinese who in the early 1880s established a fish saltery at the mouth of the Harbour in the area that became known as Irvines Landing, after its second settler, a bearded, pipe-smoking Englishman named Charlie Irvine. Irvine built a log-cabin trading post there before leaving to take in the Klondike gold rush, then in 1904 sold to the pair who really put Pender Harbour on the map—"Portuguese Joe" Gonzalves and his son-in-law Theodore (Steve) Dames. Gonzalves and Dames took advantage of the harbour's other chief resource—shelter—and established a full-blown steamer stop complete with deep-sea dock, general store, post office and hotel-saloon. Under their stewardship Pender Harbour became the supply centre for the rich timberlands of the Northern Peninsula–Jervis Inlet–Nelson Island region, and before long other services sprang up. George Duncan started a blacksmith shop in Duncan Cove, and Harry Dusenbury started another one on Dusenbury Island, which also served as the home base for a sealing schooner he owned in partnership with a gnarly old salt named Sandy McLean. McLean was touted as the original of Wolf Larsen in Jack London's novel *The Sea Wolf*. A one-armed ex-machinist named Robert Donley established a chicken ranch on Edgecombe Island in 1912, and on October 26 of that year fathered the first male child of European parentage born in the area, William Emmond Donley. Herring continued to play a role, as several salteries brought in their own crews of Scots fishermen, and Donley started a kippering operation and store at his new Donley Landing location. Farming arrived when a family of industrious German immigrants named Klein eyed the sedgy marshland at the head of the harbour and began laboriously erecting hand-built dykes against the tide, planting the salty estuary to sugar beets, berries, spuds and oysters.

Actually the oysters were introduced in 1923 by a Vancouver doctor named MacKechnie, who wanted to find something his son Ian could handle, and thought oysters might be the ticket. These were not the area's natural oysters. Scattered chips of native oyster shell can been found in the middens of old Kalpalin but *Ostea lurida*, the original oyster on this coast, was so small and scarce as to have limited value as a food source. The larger Pacific oyster, *Crassotrea gigas*, was widely cultivated in Japan, and an experiment in Ladysmith Harbour before the First World War showed it could survive in at least some BC waters.

Dr. MacKechnie was able to buy oyster seed from Japan and plant it on the tidal flats at the head of Pender Harbour, a place now known as Oyster Bay. The idea was just to fatten the oysters for slaughter, since they were not expected to reproduce in the colder BC waters. Ian's job was to oyster-sit, but he found bivalves slow company and began spending his time around the local pub, where trading fresh baking for beer provided more immediate gratification.

William Klein's old oyster farm in Pender Harbour, afterward operated for many years by the Bremer family. Farm is across Oyster Bay from site where Ian MacKechnie's pioneer experiment in oyster culture proved a "runaway" success.

Abandoned to their own devices, his oysters found a way to do what comes naturally despite the climatic obstacles and began multiplying in vast numbers. Overnight the local beaches around Pender Harbour took on a scabby appearance not even the eldest Sechelt elder had ever seen before. It was as if there had been a bumper crop of barnacles, except that when you looked closely you found it was dime-sized baby oysters the rocks were plastered with. There was some indignation directed toward that damnfool MacKechnie for making it so swimmers couldn't find a place to stand that wouldn't cut their feet, and there were many predictions of dire consequences that would come as a result of messing so massively with Mother Nature. But as the dime-sized babies grew to dollar bill-sized adults, people began to believe, even drawing parallels to the story of manna from heaven. The Kleins, whose land surrounded Oyster

Bay, soon added oysters to their varied list of cash crops, and oyster picking joined salal picking as a source of survival money for those between paycheques. Visitors from across the water took sackfulls of oysters back to their home beaches, where they continued to multiply, and by the 1950s the entire shoreline of Georgia Strait was studded with the succulent mollusks. The MacKechnie beds meanwhile petered out and Ian moved on to other escapades, but he always looked back with pride on his oyster venture, saying it was a runaway success.

Like their neighbours to the south, Pender Harbour settlers slowly came around to the realization that forestry was the region's real economic destiny. Small outfits and handloggers probably began fussing at the seaside stands as early as the 1870s, but it wasn't until 1905 that Sweden's answer to perpetual motion, the peripatetic P.B. Anderson, set up 100-man railroad camps in the area, first a few miles south of Pender at Silver Sands, then in the head of the harbour, where he high-graded the towering Douglas-fir forest on the lower slopes of the Caren Range. As a crumbling host of high-notched stumps attest, this was some of the most sublime coniferous forest on the planet, with the kind of Douglas-fir trees author Stewart Holbrook must have been thinking of when he said it would take two good men and a boy just to see all the way to the top of one. It won the Klein family a contract to cut the timber used to create Lumberman's Arch—an arrangement of colossal fir logs erected in Vancouver's Stanley Park to show just how big trees could get in BC. Lumberman's Arch became a BC landmark, one of the signatures by which the province was known to the world. By the time the arch began sagging with dry rot a few decades later, there were no replacement logs to be found on the Sunshine Coast. The first-growth giants had all been cut and sent to the mills. The Sechelt Peninsula fir may have been prime in terms of quality, but the quantity was limited in comparison to the stands around Powell River or on Vancouver Island. Today the great armies of loggers who made the place jump to their tune for much of the century have dwindled to a handful of holdouts scrounging runty pecker poles the old-timers would have scorned for fenceposts, and there is only a tree here and there that offers a hint of what the originals might have been like.

As you motor up the highway or cruise along the coast you may spot the odd leaning giant spared by successive generations of fallers because it had "elephant ears"—the big bracket fungus that tells the logger the sturdy-looking trunk is actually riddled with fungus or "conk" within. To get an idea of what a whole forest of such giants might have been like, you can pull off Highway 101 at the information sign by Haslam Creek two miles south of Pender Harbour, walk a thousand feet to the north and climb down the roadbank on the ocean side, where you will find yourself standing in a tiny pocket of virgin Douglas fir averaging about five feet in diameter. Even knowing these trees were considered too runty to bother with when P.B. Anderson was running his Flat Island railroad camp nearby in 1905, they still exude a cathedral-like power to still the soul with awe. If you can imagine the hills covered with the big sisters of these trees for as far as a day's brisk hike would carry you in any direction, you can get some notion of the forest landscape that confronted the firstcomers to the region. Settlers like the Kleins were at first dismayed at the obstacle such trees presented to those whose only thought was to clear the land for farming, but eventually the trees converted them to a different survival strategy—one founded on a rich forest industry. The Klein family survived the death of their farming ambitions to provide the area with some of its classic loggers, renowned for their strength, hard work and unruliness.

At the same time the Harbour attracted its share of the other type of Sunshine Coast settler, the species who valued it for its aesthetic charm.

One of the first settlers seduced by the Harbour's saltgrass spirit was Bertrand W. Sinclair, an author of bestselling westerns who in 1920 homesteaded what has ever since been known as Sinclair Bay. His place became a hot spot for high rollers and made the Harbour a favourite among big-name writers like the spiritualist Stewart Edward White and Erle Stanley Gardner, originator of the Perry Mason industry. Sinclair stayed in Pender Harbour the rest of his life, first switching from writing westerns to novels about BC coast fishing and logging (*Poor Man's Rock*, *The Inverted Pyramid*), then giving up writing altogether to become a full-time salmon troller, which he did into his eighties. I knew him as a barnacled old salt who didn't like to be reminded he'd ever done anything but fish.

Bertrand W. Sinclair made his mark as a bestselling author of westerns in the US before moving to Pender Harbour to celebrate west coast fishing and logging in such novels as Poor Man's Rock *and* The Inverted Pyramid.

The event that earned the Harbour a place of honour on Colombo's Literary Map of Canada did not take place until 1941 when a voluptuous but dispirited-looking twenty-eight-year old blonde stepped off the *Lady Cynthia* at Irvines Landing and asked if there were a cabin she might rent for a few months. Bill Matier, the dipsomaniac wharfinger, fixed her up in the old Irvines Landing schoolhouse and tried to make friends, but Elizabeth Smart was preoccupied with other matters. She never explained exactly how she chose Pender Harbour for her nine-month stopover, saying she just stuck a pin in a map, but she must have done enough investigating to determine it had a hospital. Whatever she thought, she was probably directed here by the same forces that washed up all the other eccentrics, for she was surely one.

According to her diary, she came equipped with "trunkfulls of evening dresses and books" and admittedly "knew nothing about practical matters." On her first shopping trip to the Irvines Landing General Store she raised eyebrows by ordering ten pounds of tea, but nothing else that would contribute to a square meal. She couldn't be bothered to keep her stove going in the drafty shack, but played her wind-up phonograph nonstop and plastered her room with cut-out pictures of madonnas, Christs, and bits of Blake and Ecclesiastes. Police officers who came to look in on her pronounced her "a harmless religious maniac." She had one visitor, a dashing young Brit with a roving eye and a thirst for booze whom she welcomed by painting her door yellow and decorating her high stilted balcony with dozens of silver cans of bright yellow dandelions, daisies and daffodils. He stayed a few weeks in April, then left her to wander alone along the bush trails and beaches in terrific distress, stumbling about, oblivious to others, talking to herself and throwing herself down on the moss and weeping inconsolably. By summer it was clear she was well advanced in pregnancy.

Viv Pieper, the woman behind the counter at the store, blurted out one day, "You're in a bad way, aren't you my dear? You're in quite a spot?"

"Oh no, thank you, I'm fine."

She tried to give the impression she was married, calling herself "Mrs. Barker," but was franker in her diary, writing on the eve of giving birth to her child, "I hope he will not mind being a bastard. Surely it will help him to avoid the bores, the snobs, the petty, & the afraid."

To local people Smart herself seemed a snob, but nobody could accuse her of being petty or afraid. Raised in a stiflingly proper Upper Canada family, she travelled around the world, lived in a ménage à trois in Mexico, then wound up in an artists' colony at Big Sur, California, where she had the love affair of her life with a fashionable (and married) English poet named George Barker. Barker promised to leave his wife for Smart and did make the one visit to Pender Harbour in April, but only left her more heartbroken than ever. In her diary Smart wrote, "I am dissolved dissolved dissolved with my tears overflowing all Pender Harbour."

She relieved her desperation by pouring it into writing, producing a work of such rhapsodic intensity it has become a classic expression of forsaken love and one of the most celebrated Canadian novels of all time, *By Grand Central Station I Sat Down and Wept*.

Whatever unseen hand had directed Smart to Harbour shores had some years earlier brought another woman who was Smart's match both in cultured background and rebellious spirit. Maximiliane von Upani Southwell was a titled Austrian aristocrat who had chucked the debutante scene in Vienna and somehow ended up living with her invalid husband and ten-year-old son in the Klein family's original log cabin at the head of Oyster Bay, "on the dole, but with immense elegance." Southwell of all people could understand what Smart was going through and took the younger woman into her cramped shack, nursing her through the final stages of her book and her pregnancy both. *By Grand Central Station I Sat Down and Wept* was finished just two weeks before Georgina Barker was born in St. Mary's Hospital on August 28, 1941. Though the book gives no credit to "this little place, mostly inhabited by people on the dole, remittance men, etc." for producing the soul-mate who saved the author's life, the novel is dedicated to Maxie Southwell, and they remained lifelong friends.

The two women returned to Pender Harbour in 1970 to revisit the place that inspired Smart to her one flash of genius. They found that her old schoolhouse had been knocked down but that the hospital where Dr. Keith Johnson had delivered the love-child of her legendary affair was still operating, although it was soon replaced by the present facility in Sechelt. The old hospital building survives today as a charming heritage resort called the Sundowner Inn. The Klein's log homestead where Smart finished her book under Maxie Southwell's care also survives, an unrecognized literary monument hunching amid the salmonberry canes and surrounded by the tidal mud of Smeshalin from which the Great Spirit had fashioned the first Kalpalin man, according to Sechelt elder Clarence Joe. As for Maxie, she bought a piece of beachfront next to Hubert Evans in Roberts Creek and spent the rest of her life on the Sunshine Coast, creatively loafing.

These days the balance between those drawn to Pender Harbour mainly for a living and those drawn by the glorious setting has tilted in favour of the latter, although there are plenty who appreciate both. Oldtimers are never done marveling at the way newcomers move in to get away from the city but do their best to bring it with them in the form of lawn sprinkling, high fences, security lights, foreshore leases, and the mindset that goes with all of that.

LEAVING PENDER HARBOUR BY BOAT, THE FIRST thing you bump into is Nelson Island. If you leave by car, you may never hear of it. Nelson Island is the Gulf island nobody knows even though it's bigger than Bowen, Gabriola or Lasqueti. As a product of Nelson Island myself I have to admit to a bit of personal hangup about this, one symptom of which is that anything I write longer than five hundred words is likely to mention Nelson Island at least once. But I'm not the only one to experience a twinge of defensiveness. Local historian Karen Southern, when preparing her excellent little book *The Nelson Island Story*, at first considered calling it *Not Just a Lot of Rock and Christmas Trees*.

Those who deny Nelson Island its rightful place often claim nobody lives there. In fact, Nelson has been continuously occupied about as long as any other part of the Sunshine Coast, at least since the early 1890s when an English school teacher named John Wray landed with his wife Sarah and five children at Hidden Bay on the west side of the island. True, the advantages of Nelson Island life were not apparent to Sarah immediately, but she was a town girl born and bred whose entire wilderness experience before following her husband into darkest British Columbia consisted of two visits to the English seashore. One day when John came home from getting the mail (obviously no five-minute chore), he found her waiting with all their possessions packed and an ultimatum on her lips: "I want to get out of here right now." John must have been a good talker. He moved, but only a few miles down the beach to Quarry Bay, where the granite quarry offered steady wages and at least some society. Forty years later John and Sarah were still married and still living on Nelson Island, progenitors of a numerous clan that did much to tame the Sunshine Coast.

The full-time Nelson population has not always been able to claim quantity, the average being somewhere under twenty-five, but quality ought to count for something. I have already mentioned that this was the island Harry Roberts sought refuge on after fleeing the overdevelopment of Roberts Creek in 1930. One of his neighbours was a sister of the outlaw Jesse James, who is remembered for firing shots across the bow of the steamer *Comox* when she wanted it to call on her rancherie near Quarry Bay. (Most settlers were satisfied simply to hoist a flag.)

Nelson Island has not lacked for major industries, although things have slowed since the end of World War One. It may be all rock and Christmas trees, but the rock is damn fine rock. The island's earliest developers made a virtue of adversity by turning the whole west side of the island into a series of stone quarries, and Nelson Island granite found its way into the Vancouver Art Gallery, both Vancouver post offices, the BC legislative buildings and a million or so headstones.

The island had a salmon cannery once, down near Green Bay on the east side, which is curious since there are no major salmon runs in that neighbourhood. Ian MacKechnie, the oyster pioneer, explained it to me by pointing out that during a world war "you can can anything that swims." His view is supported by the fact that at the war's end the cannery was quickly converted into a shingle mill, then later into an extremely low budget summer resort. This was not the island's first tourist facility. Back near the turn of the century a visionary named John West had built a seventeen-room hotel on Agamemnon Channel, which he christened Westmere Lodge. On opening night he had one guest, and it went downhill from there. Later reports find Mr. West sawing his hotel in half and using the lumber thus liberated to heat the remaining half. Island people are not always practical, but they are tenacious. The good half of Westmere Lodge is still functioning.

Leaving Pender Harbour by car, you follow Highway 101 around the Peninsula's largest and most popular lakes, Sakinaw and Ruby, before pausing for another ferry ride at Earls Cove, once the homestead of the Earl family, whom I remember for nothing so much as their amazing way of talking. Living alone in a place that was a paragon of wilderness isolation before the government abruptly turned it into a mass transit depot, the Earls developed one of the most picturesque drawls to be encountered this side of the Ozarks. Come to think of it, their neighbour Olli Sladey, the Sechelt Peninsula's first millionaire, had a way of squeezing all the juice out of his vowels, too. It gives you an inkling of how quickly a local dialect can get started. The Earl boys' parents were English and Olli's Finnish, but by the time civilization caught up with them halfway through their second generation on the site, the two families were well on their way to concocting a new variety of spoken English. There was lots of that in the old days. The fishermen in Pender Harbour had their own sound. The gillnetters, that is. Net-men were more communal, whereas the trollers, being off by themselves most of the time, tended to develop one-man dialects. People from different areas would invent their own words. One I remember from Powell River is *zunga*, for the rope you use to swing out over a swimming hole. Everybody up there says it, but I never heard it anywhere else.

EGMONT, A VILLAGE OF ABOUT 250 DOWN a three-mile side road just before the ferry terminal, is something of a throwback to a time of traditional gumboot customs though even here, modern currents are fast erasing the old sounds, smells and sights.

Like Pender Harbour and so many of the smaller, older settlements, Egmont was made up of big, extended families—the Jeffries, the Silveys, the Griffiths, the Vaughans, the Wests. The Silveys especially, descendants of a Portuguese trader named Joseph Silvia who ran the first saloon in Vancouver and in 1868 fathered the first child with European content born in that city, personify the community's distinctive salal brush roots.

Egmont is also like Pender Harbour in the way it defies rational town planning by rambling along the beach from bay to point to cove, as roads twist and turn maniacally to keep up. Egmont is a little like one of those prairie towns bisected by railyards, except in this case the divider is a busy marine thoroughfare called Sechelt Narrows. Old Egmont on the north side of the inlet is accessible only by water, giving docks, boardwalks, beaching grids, kicker boats and water taxis a prominence that recalls the earlier days of many coastal communities. A careful observer will note that Egmont's waterfront has a somewhat more battened-down look in comparison to Pender, owing to the heavy currents flowing in and out of Skookumchuck Rapids, just down the inlet.

The Skookumchuck experience, along with touring Princess Louisa Inlet (also accessible from Egmont), is one of the must-do's of visiting the Sunshine Coast, although it can be rather anti-climactic if you don't time your visit to catch a big tide at full rip. Even then, it may strike you as not much different than a patch of moderately white water on a medium-sized river. What the chuck does that no river does is slam into reverse every six hours, and you can't experience its full eeriness without observing a whole cycle from spin to soak to spin again. Even that is nothing beside the death-defying thrill of venturing into its smoking maw in some sort of vessel, keeping in mind that about a dozen people that we know of have died doing this. The total is likely to keep increasing as the chuck grows more popular with whitewater kayakers and other addicts of the extreme.

Netsheds, barn-like structures built at the very edge of the tide for storing and mending fishermen's nets, once crowded the Pender Harbour shoreline but are now vanishing.

Great Blue Herons adapt well to modern life and often haunt busy marinas and fuel docks, ever watchful for an unprotected bait tank.

Sport fishing for salmon has long been one the Sunshine Coast's chief attractions.

Opposite: View over Gerrans Bay from Lowe's Resort in Madeira Park. Thunderbird totem has an unusual history, having been carved by an airline pilot as an anniversary gift for his wife.

US journalist Edith Iglauer came to Pender Harbour to do a story on salmon troller John Daly for The New Yorker, married him, wrote the west coast classic Fishing With John, and stayed on as a confirmed Sunshine Coaster after Daly died. Here she shares a laugh with her son Jay at the Daly homestead in Garden Bay.

Retired Pender Harbour towboater and aviation buff Bill Thompson poses with his latest hobby, a restored US Navy biplane.

The government wharf at Madeira Park is still one of the busiest places in town.

Right: How did they get it up there? Rusted remains of a logging donkey precariously balanced on bluff near the mouth of Pender Harbour attest to the ingenuity of early loggers. Once denounced as unsightly, ruin is now a much-photographed landmark.

Like many coastal villages where all business took place at the water's edge, early Pender Harbour was laced together with wooden boardwalks. This one at Garden Bay was named Greene Walk in honour of pioneer Anglican missionary Canon Alan Greene.

Above: On those rare winters when it becomes cold enough to freeze Pender Harbour's many lakes, everybody takes a break to go skating.

Ruby Lake in winter.

Top: Classic wooden tug the Nanaimo Tillicum all decked out for annual Christmas carolling cruise around Pender Harbour.

Above: Pender Harbour has no theatre, but country life can have its compensations. Here school kids joyride in a herring skiff.

Following pages: Unnamed Pender Harbour islet glows in foreground as sun sets over Malaspina Strait.

Peggy Connor, longtime chairperson of the Sunshine Coast Regional District, takes a moment to glean some pearls of wisdom from Egmont wharfinger Vera Grafton (right).

Billy Griffith takes the floor with daughter Maureen as Egmont turns out in force to mark a wedding in one of its leading families.

Egmont, the northernmost settlement on the Sechelt Peninsula, retains much of the salty flavour that characterized coast life of earlier times. It was founded in 1880s by a legendary half-Scots, half-Portuguese seaman named Joseph Silvey, whose descendents still live in the area.

Opposite: Classic wooden seiner Silversides, owned by Leonard Silvey, looms out of mist at Egmont dock.

*Skipper George Weeks grimaces as his sloop
Moonchild heels over in a tidal whirlpool.*

*Left: Whitewater kayaker defies the whirlpools to
surf on standing wave in Skookumchuck Rapids.*

*Below: Skookumchuck Rapids at Egmont presents
an awesome spectacle on a big flood tide.*

Egmont fisherman Billy Griffith's waterfront home is equipped with its own wharf, shipyard and netshed (left), all important for keeping up the family's fleet. Below: The Tzoonie River, one of the Griffith's two seineboats.

Part Four

Jervis
Inlet

Malibu Lodge at the entrance to Princess Louisa Inlet was built as a luxury resort for Hollywood movie stars but ended up serving as an affordable summer youth camp operated by Young Life, a non-denominational Christian organization.

JERVIS INLET, WHICH ZIGZAGS deep into the Coast Range like a forty-mile lightning bolt between the Peninsula and the Powell River side, is a classic coastal fjord, shadowed most of its length by mile-high mountain walls. It is very deep. A marker buoy is anchored about mid-stream offshore of St. Vincent Bay, and you often see pleasure boats giving it a wide berth, no doubt thinking that, like most marker buoys, this one must indicate treacherous shallows. In fact it indicates the greatest depth of water to be found on the Inside Passage, a 3,000-foot hole known as "the Jervis Deep." It is marked because the US military has confiscated it for testing deep-water weaponry.

Actually I think of this wide gulf between the mainland and Nelson Island as pre-inlet, although it's shown on the maps as all one with Jervis. It's not until you round Foley Head and begin ascending the long crack in the mountains that you start getting that claustrophobic feeling I associate with the real Jervis Inlet. As the nervous skipper I am, I always find this part of the inlet a little menacing from the vantage point of a small boat. Just as Howe Sound has a resident typhoon called the Squamish, Jervis has an even meaner one called the Jervis Express and it has a habit of cooking up on short notice. The sheer cliffs afford no shelter, and the inlet's deep bottom is littered with rickety camp tenders, fishboats and the bones of luckless gyppo loggers who failed to show proper respect for the volatile local weathers. There are a few places where the steep-to shores relax into a brief dent of river mouth, at Vancouver Bay, Brittain River and Deserted Bay, but even these places offer dubious refuge.

The parts of Jervis that are not bare granite bluff speckled with mountain goats were once thickly forested with fir and cedar, but now offer a case study in the effects of bad logging practices. The hillsides above Egmont Point at the entrance to the inlet proper have regained some of their green cover after being clear-cut twenty or thirty years ago, but a mass of ugly brown washouts that snake down sometimes five hundred feet bear witness to the risks involved in building logging roads on steep slopes. On the opposite side of the inlet great barren patches can be seen where the timber has failed to regenerate three decades after logging, and the hillside north of Brittain River remains scruffy from a logging-related forest fire in the 1950s. Elsewhere, in the broad valleys of the Vancouver and Deserted rivers, the great Douglas-fir stands that spawned big railway camps early in the century have surged back with such profusion the sites are choked with stunted, undersized timber which is prey to a host of diseases and parasites. It is to bring an end to such environmental degradation that the provincial NDP government clamped down on destructive logging practices with its 1995 Forest Practices Code.

THE FEATURE THAT SETS JERVIS APART FROM ITS sister inlets occurs ten miles from the head on the east side. There the mountain walls unexpectedly part and let into a four-mile side inlet surrounded by such precipitous bluffs the effect is like looking up at the sky from the bottom of a colossal and extremely gorgeous cavern. "There is no use describing that inlet," Erle Stanley Gardner once wrote, before proceeding to ignore his own advice. "There is a calm tranquility which stretches from the smooth surface of the reflecting waters straight up into

Sheer cliff in Princess Louisa Inlet known as "Echo Rock."

infinity. The deep calm of eternal silence is only disturbed by the muffled roar of throbbing waterfalls as they plunge down from sheer cliffs. There is no scenery in the world that can beat it. Not that I've seen the rest of the world. I don't need to. I've seen Princess Louisa Inlet."

I won't fall into the trap of trying to describe Princess Louisa except to say few Sunshine Coasters would deny it is the Hope Diamond of the area's scenic jewels. It is the place we take those special visitors we want to hook on the coast, the one experience guaranteed to jar the most jaded soul into a full-blown state of awe. I have been visiting Princess Louisa regularly since I was a kid and it never seems enough. Despite going in many different weathers, moods and ages, it has never failed to send me away with a renewed sense of life's promise.

The inlet's rare magnetism draws remarkable people to it and inspires them to extraordinary exertions. Legend has it that it was avoided by the Sechelt after a small village at the head was buried by one of the inlet's periodic rockslides, but band elder Clarence Joe claimed his people used to visit it for recreational purposes just as the white man would later.

Princess Louisa was ignored by the muckers early on because its only substantial resource was beauty, which didn't readily lend itself to being canned or milled—a challenge inventor Thomas Hamilton would apply himself to later.

Herman Casper just wanted to wake up in the morning and see it. Casper was a deserter from the German army who homesteaded the only decently flat land in the area, the peninsula down at the inlet mouth by Malibu Rapids, in 1900. When he wasn't black-smithing for local handloggers, Casper whiled away his days spoiling his twenty-six cats and composing songs in praise of the magnificent surroundings, which he was happy to perform with his zither for visiting boaters:

Beyond Mount Alfred, in ze vest
Where ze sun goes down to rest
It draws me dere, I don' know vy
S'pose it is ze colour in ze sky.
For zey are purple, mauve and pink
Howeber it makes me vunder, look, and t'ink.

Casper was followed by Charles (Daddy) Johnstone, a towering mountain man from Daniel Boone country who kept edging west ahead of civilization until he and his six family landed up at Princess Louisa around 1909. There they threw together a one-room split-cedar shack, lived off the land and had three more kids. The Johnstone gang may have succeeded in getting closer to the inlet's soul than anyone since the Sechelt in the days when they had it to themselves. As part of their education, the old

man used to send sons Steve and Judd up on the snowy plateau above Princess Louisa without jacket or shoes and only matches, salt and a jackknife for survival. They would live by their wits for weeks at a time, and explore miles into the interior of the province. After World War One Daddy began to feel even Jervis was too cramped and carried on to Alaska, where he became famous as "Handlogger Johmstone." But Steve and Judd returned and passed the rest of their days in homage to the fabulous Jervis landscape that had been so deeply imprinted on them in their formative years. Their names became synonymous with the inlet's wild spirit and Judd in particular became famous for his tall tales of pioneer times.

Judd married Dora Jeffries from Egmont and stayed up Princess Louisa through the birth of their first three girls, sixty miles from the nearest family. The sun would disappear behind the inlet crags for two months in the depths of winter and it would get so cold the salt water would freeze from shore to shore. To get anything that couldn't be obtained from the bush Judd would have to drag the boat across two miles of sea ice and row to Pender Harbour, a hundred-mile round trip. He was always a welcome sight at Portuguese Joe's bar in Irvines Landing and never had to pay for a drink. All you had to do was ask him how things were going.

"Could be worse. Had a hard blow and a cedar tree come down on the shack is all."

"Very big?"

"Naw, only about six foot on the butt."

"Good God, Judd. Didn't it do a lot of damage?"

"Naw. Fell crost the bed right where the old woman was sleepin', but it hung up on the stove before it could git 'er. Tore the roof off is all."

"That's terrible, Judd!"

"Naw. I just took a couple blocks off the end and split up a mess o' shakes. Old woman bin after me fer a new roof anyways."

"What about the rest of the tree. How did you remove it?"

"Didn't bother. It was pointin' in the stove anyways, so I jus' lit the fire and stuck the Gilchrist jack on the other end. Every time the old woman wanted some exter heat, I just hollered at the kid to go out and give a few clicks on the jack. It was auto-feed, like."

"So it wasn't so bad after all."

"Hell no. I got a new roof and a whole winter's heat without once havin' to leave the shack."

I sometimes wonder if it was due to Judd Johnstone that the entire Jervis Inlet–Nelson Island area seemed to become such a prime bullshit producing zone. When I was growing up there it seemed you couldn't get a straight answer out of anybody.

Certainly you couldn't get one out of James (Mac) Macdonald, the globetrotting American playboy who fell under the Princess's spell in 1919. "After travelling around the world and seeing many of its famous beauty spots, I felt I was well able to evaluate the magnificence of Princess Louisa," he wrote in one of his more sober utterances. "This place had to equal or better anything I had seen."

Like many another wealthy American who no sooner spied a thing of beauty in a foreign land than he had to have it, Macdonald promptly applied to the BC government to purchase the inlet head, and the government turned out to be eager to unload it. Their appraisal of the 292-acre site, which would come to be called "The Eighth Wonder of the World" and attract 20,000 gawkers a season despite its inaccessibility, was that only 42 acres were flat enough to be of any use, so Macdonald could have the whole thing for $420, if that wasn't asking too much. He took possession in 1927.

Through absolutely no fault of its own, this turned out to be the best thing the government could have done. Within a few years Macdonald would be turning down $400,000 offers from hotel chains and preserving the area for public use with a determination the government would not come to appreciate until 1964, when Macdonald finally had the satisfaction of seeing his beloved charge consecrated as a Class A Marine Park.

Rich, eloquent and handsome, "Mac" Macdonald could have had his pick of successful careers, but from his fateful encounter with the Princess in the prime of his life until the day he could no longer hobble around on his own, he devoted his entire existence to being her chief admirer, protector and ambassador to the world. He got married in 1939, but the new wife made the mistake of forcing him to choose between the Princess and her, and a Mexican divorce quickly followed.

Mac left the inlet only during the winter months, when the weather becomes much harsher than the coastal norm. At first he rented a *pied à terre* in Pender Harbour from his friend Bertrand Sinclair, and later he established regular winter digs in Acapulco. From May to October he was back at Princess Louisa, continuing his endless study of her moods, cataloguing her wonders and expounding on them to visitors. In time every feature in the inlet, from Chatterbox Falls to Trapper's Rock, came to be known by a name Mac gave it. He became a walking encyclopedia of inlet history and lore, most of it unreliable, but all of it highly entertaining.

Macdonald's presence became an attraction in itself, compelling regulars like John Barrymore to return year after year to pass long evenings sitting on the afterdeck of his splendiferous MV *Infanta*, where Mac would tell stories and point out faces in the rock formations of the bluffs.

(Barrymore claimed to have discovered Napoleon, though Mac later speculated you had to be drinking Napoleon brandy to see it). Hollywood types seemed to take a particular shine to Mac. At various times he entertained the likes of Ronald Colman, William Powell, and Mack Sennett, complete with his entourage of bathing beauties, who filmed part of a movie called *Alaskan Love Song* in the inlet, but he was equally attentive to locals and kids, reputedly turning down dinner with Arthur Godfrey so he could keep a storytelling date at the youth camp. This is all the more notable considering Mac's legendary appetite for free grub. It is said that from the time the first yacht showed up in the spring to the time the last one left in the fall, he never ate his own cooking.

Macdonald was a great admirer of Judd Johnstone and, after Judd moved south to Hardy Island, of his brother Steve, who stayed up-inlet all his life. He was also a great fan of old Casper. During one of his winters south, Macdonald hired some professional musicians to make a record of Casper's songs, which proved a great hit among inlet fanciers and netted the old smithy a rare spot of cash. Macdonald was outraged in 1940 when aviation tycoon Thomas Hamilton talked Casper into parting with his beloved acreage for $500 so he could build a luxury resort called Malibu Lodge. Mac cheered when Malibu went broke in 1947 and was taken over by Young Life, a non-denominational church group offering low-budget vacations to city kids.

Macdonald was particularly attentive to Muriel Blanchet, the adventuring Victoria widow who cruised the inlet with her five children in the 1930s. With the help of Hubert Evans she recorded her experiences in the coastal classic *The Curve of Time*, which has a lengthy passage describing Mac as "the Man from California," which of course he wasn't. He also kept up a kind of friendly bullshitting competition with Tom Brazil, caretaker of the Macomber estate on Hardy Island down south at the mouth of Jervis Inlet, who had a troupe of tame deer and entertained boaters with a repertoire of tall tales and bogus lore that rivalled Mac's. Mac would arrange for southbound boaters to stop in and give Brazil the latest news from Princess Louisa—for instance, that Mac had narrowly escaped being killed by a cougar which leapt at him from behind a tree and would have got him but for Mac's quick side-jump, an uncanny move he had perfected in his college football days. Following the attack, the story went, Mac heard some crashing in the bush, and here was the cougar, hopping back and forth practicing his football move.

Brazil would have a few days to think about that before sending the next boat north with the latest news from Hardy Island, perhaps about his bear, the one he had raised from a cub and taught to do odd jobs around

Ancient rock paintings in Jervis Inlet have lasted centuries on surfaces that obliterate the best modern paints after a few years. Mystery of how images were applied and what they mean remains unsolved.

Below: According to popular lore, Deserted Bay got its name when smallpox wiped out the large Native village of Tsonai. Steel barge abandoned in modern times adds resonance to the name.

the place. In fact he had nicknamed this bear "Mac," because it was so effective mooching grub from visiting boats. One day he needed the bear to skid a wood log out of the bush, but call as he would, he couldn't raise it. Then he saw something big and black rooting around in a berry patch and whistled the special signal that meant "time to saddle up," but the bear ignored him. Tom had to beat it on the snout with a knotty fir branch before he could climb on its back, and even then the bear proved to be in such an ornery mood he could hardly stay aboard. They were both covered with lumps by the time they finally got the log skidded down to the woodshed. No sooner were they unhitched than another bear came staggering out of the shed and gave Tom a big lick on the face. It was only then he realized his pet bear had been sleeping in the woodshed the whole time. The one he'd been riding was a wild one that had strayed by.

Sometimes Mac would resort to composing his ripostes on paper. On September 12, 1941 he sent a boat down-inlet carrying this letter:

My Dear Mr. Brazil,

Last week I had a visit from Corp. Allen of Powell River who stated that he had visited Hardy Island recently and that while he was walking across the island he had seen a peculiar looking animal half man and half beast lurking in the woods. The Corporal immediately concluded that it must be one of your African offspring that was visiting you—and not wishing to embarrass you did not mention the matter to you. I questioned the Corporal concerning the man-beast and immediately realized that it was my very valuable Orang-utan which I had imported from Sumatra several years ago at great expense.

Mount Churchill behind Vancouver Bay dominates the lower reaches of Jervis Inlet.

As I am growing into the sunset years of life and no longer have the strength or stamina to climb the mountains and milk the wild goats before breakfast, I have trained this animal to perform that chore for me, so you can readily understand how much I miss my Orang-utan and how tired I am getting of canned milk.

Now Mr. Brazil, I am not accusing you of theft for I know you to be a man of upright character—at least, that is the reputation your children have given you, and I have met a lot of them in the South Seas, China, Africa, and in Borneo. How you obtained my Orang-utan I don't know, but I want you to return him *immediately*. I suggest that you have him properly caged and charter a boat and send him up here accompanied by Mr. Forrest (Judd) Johnstone or some other reputable animal trainer. If you send Mr. Johnstone along with my animal please put a label around Mr. Johnstone's neck so that I shall know which is the Orang-utan.

Very truly yours,
James Macdonald

Under the inlet's influence Macdonald became one of the most ardent apostles of the creed that humanity was placed on the Sunshine Coast "not to be doing but to be." He even went so far as to dedicate himself formally to "the satisfying state of loaferhood."

"The world needs ten million full time thinking loafers dedicated to the purpose of bringing this cockeyed life back to its normal balance," he declared in his five-point manifesto of loaferdom.

Of course it helped to be the favourite son of a Seattle grocery heiress, a fact Macdonald made no bones about, advising would-be loafers: "Before birth, look the field over and pick out a family in which some member has misspent his life in amassing sufficient do-re-me to permit you to dodge the squirrel cage." In this he differs

from the Johnstone boys, who would argue that you could enjoy the best the coast had to offer with no more accumulated assets than a jackknife and a box of matches.

I remember Mac as a pleasant old man with a crown of luminous silver hair who used to keep his houseboat the *Seaholm* in Madeira Park while he waited for the inlet to thaw in the spring. I had a paper route, and while it was a bit of nuisance to paddle over to where he was anchored, it was always worth seeing what nonsense he would come up with. One spring he launched into a big production about a new sport which had taken Acapulco beaches by storm that season, and ceremoniously produced this wonderful innovation he'd smuggled back just for my benefit. I was excited by the buildup but disappointed by the actual item, which looked like the lid off a small garbage can. He said you flicked it so it sort of hovered like a flying saucer. He made me practise it with him until I had the knack, then commanded me to go off and spread the fad among my friends. That was how Madeira Park became the first Canadian beachhead of the Frisbee craze, away back in 1957. To a twelve-year-old, Mac seemed like nothing so much as a great big overaged kid, which I am sure is a judgment he would have been most delighted to accept. The only thing you had to watch is that he didn't lure you inside his cabin and try to make you play chess. As a chess fanatic he was known for his willingness to play with anyone, no matter how incompetent, but I am sad to say even his legendary patience was checkmated in my case.

Mac died in a Seattle rest home in 1978. His ashes are planted inside a boulder at the head of Princess Louisa, beneath an inscription which reads "Laird of the inlet, Gentleman, friend to all who came here."

Looking into fabled Princess Louisa Inlet from the mouth.

Second-growth forest crowds water's edge near Princess Louisa Inlet.

Top: Aerial view of Malibu rapids and Malibu Resort.

Following pages: Chatterbox Falls provides a focus for the breathtaking scenery at the head of Princess Louisa Inlet.

Part Four

The Powell River Area

Begun as a company town in 1908, modern Powell River was created in 1955 when the communities of Wildwood, Westview and Cranberry Lake amalgamated with the original company townsite to form the District of Powell River. By the mid-1990s the District had a population of 15,000 and the whole area, 20,000.

A FRIEND OF MINE WHO works for one of the big forest companies had to travel up the coast recently explaining some new joint government–industry strategy and was quite struck with the difference between the north side of Jervis Inlet and the south in attitudes about logging and industrial progress in general. The meetings on the lower coast were big noisy affairs overflowing with well-prepared critics of all philosophical shades, where the upper coast meetings were small, businesslike and supportive.

"Boy that's a cranky area you live in," she said rather accusingly, as if harbouring a suspicion I might be part of the problem (completely unfounded). She came to the meeting prepared for a barrage of green-think, which she got, but was blindsided by a bellicose business agent for the loggers' union who attacked her for being too green herself. "They were coming at us from every direction," she said. "But it's a different world up Powell River way. They like jobs up there."

To cross over to the north side of the inlet is to leave the spirit of genteel loaferdom behind. The forty-mile coastline between the ferry dock at Saltery Bay and the terminus of Highway 101 at Lund, which local residents break into some ten distinct communities while lower coasters lump them all together as Powell River, is presided over by an industrious spirit that tends to be impatient with those who lack the Protestant work ethic.

This is perhaps unavoidable given the great resource wealth of the area, which has made it much more of an industrial zone than the lower coast. My father has always maintained that Powell River is a better place to live than the crank-infested lower coast, but given that he thinks both Harry Roberts and Mac Macdonald were self-regarding layabouts, I suppose that isn't too surprising.

The principal determining factor in Powell River history is that broad stretch of low-elevation real estate lying inland of the coast between Stillwater and Lund, roughly forty miles square, which supported a forest comparable in quality to that on the Sechelt Peninsula but vaster in volume.

From the 1890s onward the Powell Forest attracted many of the major forest companies of the time, including the venerable Hastings Mill Company of Vancouver at Lang Bay and Wildwood; Bloedel, Stewart & Welch of Bellingham at Myrtle Point; Lamb Lumber Company then Brooks, Scanlon & O'Brien of Minnesota at Stillwater; and Merrill & Ring of Seattle in Theodosia Inlet. Between 1896 and 1955, when the Eagle River and Northern Railway pulled up the area's last functioning trackage, the Powell River area was one of the great centres of steam railway logging, with 20 locomotives and 300 cars running on over 100 miles of track. Camps in the area housed more than a thousand men. Little trace of this activity remains

The "Hulks," a string of war-surplus cargo ships used as a breakwater for the pulp mill booming ground, are a Powell River landmark.

except enormous crumbling stumps and an old steam locomotive reputed to be rusting in peace somewhere beyond the head of Lewis Lake. The timber giant MacMillan Bloedel still employs some eighty men at its Stillwater Division and Andy Byrne's Granet Lake show keeps another couple dozen off the street, but the total complement of loggers still active in the area has likely dwindled to fewer than two hundred.

Just the same, the area still carries the stamp of the big timber era on its soul. At the turn of the century, as settlers from the Gibsons family down at Gibsons Landing to the Thulins up at Lund were consolidating their footholds in the coastal forest, the stretch of shoreline where Powell River and Westview repose today was unsettled slash. Across Malaspina Strait, Texada Island was booming with its twin cities of Vananda and Texada City, and up the coast at Lund the Thulin brothers were already building their second hotel, but the only permanent resident along the Powell River shore was a squatter from Missouri named Tom Ogburn. Ogburn had crisscrossed the continent looking for the perfect wilderness home, and circa 1900 he built his log cabin at the top of the falls on Powell River.

Poor Tom. In 1907 he woke up to find a railroad rumbling past his back door as the Michigan and Puget Logging Company established their pioneering 2.5-mile line from the lake to the beach, later extended to what is now known as Willingdon Beach Park. But even that disturbance would soon seem minor. In 1908 the Brooks Scanlon company decided the area's vast timber wealth, combined with the hydroelectric potential of the spectacular falls that thundered undammed onto the beach, made Powell River a likely spot to establish one of western Canada's first pulp and paper mills. Tom's cabin was soon in the middle of a roaring construction site as the newly formed Powell River Company stripped the little valley to build its dam, mill and townsite. Unlike unsuccessful attempts at Swanson Bay and Port Mellon, the Powell River pulp mill was a winner, and after some early struggles, rapidly grew into the largest pulp and paper mill in the world, creating a prosperous new coastal city around it. By the 1940s, the bountiful local timber supply which had provided the original impetus for the mill was petering out, but the enterprise had enough momentum that it was pulling fibre in from all parts of the coast. Between 1921 and 1941 the town grew from 2,100 to 8,000 people; by 1981 it peaked at over 20,000.

This dramatic development overshadowed everything else that took place in the whole region. It does still. Even though modernization has reduced the mill workforce considerably, the local economy still experiences an earthquake every time the pulp market hiccups. The very way Powell Riverites view their universe puts the "town"

at the centre and everything else at the margins. Anything up in the direction of Lund is referred to as "north of town." Saltery Bay, Stillwater, Lang Bay and Black Point are all referred to as "south of town."

THE MOST UNUSUAL SIGHT IN SALTERY BAY AT the start of the drive into Powell River can't be viewed from the highway, or from a boat, or from anything but a wetsuit. It is a nine-foot bronze statue of a mermaid and it is located three fathoms under the sea just offshore of the Saltery Bay Campsite. It didn't fall off the ferry—it was placed there on purpose to anchor Powell River's not uncontested claim to being the "Scuba Diving Capital of Canada." The area running from Saltery Bay to Thunder Bay has long been a hot spot for underwater sightseeing, boasting an "Octopus City" and several wrecks as well as the bra-less bronze. If you want to check, you don't have to be Jacques Cousteau. This dive site is advertised as wheelchair accessible.

The Mermaid of Saltery Bay, the Canada's first underwater statue.

After snaking around the notorious Thunder Bay bluffs, the road levels out and traverses a gently sloping landscape with a southerly exposure that was surveyed into forty-acre parcels back in the 1920s when the government was still clinging to the idea that the highest use it could be put to was farming. In the words of the late Paradise Valley pioneer Roy Padgett, "They were selling it for two and a half dollars an acre for years before they realized this was forest land with second-growth timber on it worth thousands to the acre." Occasional green fields can still be seen holding out against the relentless onslaught of temperate jungle. One of the first and grandest of the forest farms can be glimpsed just as the road comes down off the bluffs where in the late 1890s Farquar McRae homesteaded most of the lush 1,500-acre peninsula that runs out to wave-swept Scotch Fir Point. He wrestled the great fir stumps out of the soil until he, like the Kleins, realized there was less money in slaugh-tering his beeves than in hitching them to trees, and so turned ox-logger. Three quarters of a century of selective logging by Farquar and his son Fraser left the vast McCrae spread more or less intact and a lot of hearts were broken when it was not made into a park after Fraser's passing. It would have given the south coast another Stanley Park.

A couple miles farther along, the highway affords a close-up view of one of the coast's most familiar land-marks, the Stillwater surge tank. The twenty-storey structure balances pressure in the mile-long penstock which carries water from the dam on Lois Lake down to the Powell River mill's auxiliary powerhouse on Stillwater Bay. Because of its placement on the hillside with full exposure to Malaspina Strait, mariners can sight the Stillwater tower clear down to Bellingham. Small boaters steering courses up the gulf have become so dependent on it as a landmark over the years that if it is ever discontinued as a surge tank, it will have to be kept up as an aid to navigation.

The Powell Forest is positively sodden with lakes and Lois River, emptying the Lois Lake–Khartoum Lake–Horseshoe Lake system, is the second largest drainage

The Stillwater surge tank, used to keep even pressure in water flowing to a nearby hydro plant, is visible for miles out in Georgia Strait.

after the Powell Lake system itself. As you whiz over the concrete viaduct that spans the Lois River gorge just a mile past the surge tank, you may wonder at stories like the one pioneer Edith Flynn told about crossing this river as a child: "The first bridge across the river was just below the present bridge, at the first curve in the river below the falls. It was made from two logs, one larger one on the high side and one smaller one on the low side so you were walking on a tilt, and it had a belly in the middle so it sloped up to the bank on either end. It was quite scary, because it was very high, and it would wobble. It had a handrail, but you didn't dare lean on it. I saw people start out walking, then get down on their hands and knees, then get scared to go any further. We kids got so used to it we didn't think anything of it." You may look over the edge of the new Lois River bridge and search in vain for the raging torrent the early settlers called the Eagle River, which once drained three lakes called the Gordon Pashas. When a wooden crib dam was built at the outlet of the first Gordon Pasha in 1930 and then replaced by a higher concrete dam in 1942, the two lower lakes were merged into one large one renamed Lois Lake. This lake serves as the jumping-off point for the Powell Forest canoe route, a spectacular and extremely well established forty-mile course which loops through twelve lakes and comes out on Powell Lake just above the river. At the same time Lois Lake was created, the river draining it was renamed the Lois River, but the name was somewhat academic since most of the water was diverted through the Stillwater penstock, leaving barely enough moisture in the old channel to wet the gravel on most days.

Either way, the water still finds its way to tidewater at Stillwater, today a tiny but deeply rooted hamlet dominated by a big MacMillan Bloedel log sorting ground. Starting in 1909, this was the base of some of the area's largest logging operations, when the US firm Brooks, Scanlon & O'Brien built a railway system reaching twenty miles back into the fabulously rich timber of the Eagle (Lois) River drainage. The land around the Gordon Pasha chain was logged using fifteen steam donkeys and two large floating camps which were towed from claim to claim. Stillwater served as the social centre of the mainland side before the Powell River mill was established in 1911, with a hotel, store and community hall to go with the big BS&O'B camp. It was this company that got the bright idea of starting the pulp and paper mill which changed the history of the whole region. Its successor, MacMillan Bloedel Ltd., still favours Stillwater with the largest logging operation in the area.

A few miles farther north Highway 101 crosses a smaller watercourse known as Lang Creek, which is still full of water and each fall is packed with hatchery-produced salmon. Lang Creek drains the third largest of the area's lake systems, Haslam Lake, and was the site of the area's first logging railway, established sometime in the 1890s by the pioneering Hastings Mill Company of Vancouver. This company was succeeded by the legendary Lamb Lumber Company, whose redoubtable leader, John Blacklock "Daddy" Lamb, was a frustrated farmer famous for getting settlers to start stumpranches in the logged-off slash along his railroads. If you want the thrill of running the family Hupmobile over one of the area's oldest logging railway beds, Zilinsky Road at Lang Bay follows the grade of Lamb's old Vancouver Timber and Trading Company Railway. This line was unique in that it was the only one of the area's big pioneer logging operations that was not operated by an American company. In 1916, the Haslam Lake Timber and Logging Company Railway, a longer line, was run up the opposite side of Lang Creek to Haslam Lake and used to load out logs dumped into the lake by operations all around its shores.

The Lang Creek–Kelly Creek–Black Point area offered the most attractive land along this shore, resulting in some of the more permanent homesteading experiments. It still retains some of the feeling of an independent community, with its own community hall and a charming picnic ground fronting the fabulous Palm Beach.

There is something uniquely striking about Myrtle Point, about five miles closer to Powell River, and it's not only that the road breaks out of the bush and at last offers the traveller a more than fleeting glimpse of Malaspina Strait. It may be the area's history. White settlement at Myrtle Point harks back before logging to the era of the fur trade, when a fur trader named Leonard Frolander set up a trading post in the 1880s, arguably the first non-Indian settlement along the Powell River shore. Frolander held sway into the late 1890s, then in 1911 the big Seattle firm Bloedel, Stewart & Welch chose the site as the saltwater base for a sprawling logging enterprise that would involve five camps stretching from nearby Paradise Valley to the side of Mount Smith at the head of Haslam Lake, twenty miles away.

Myrtle Point is one of the only big camp locations

from the glory days of steam logging where you can still see some outlines of the old works. The little islets offshore still carry remnants of the rock fill used to create a breakwater for the big BS&W booming ground, and lines of black posts in the beach mud—the stumps of rotted pilings—trace a ghostly outline of the elaborate railway trestle that used to carry the four locomotives and fifty-three log cars of the BS&W railroad out to the log dump. The flat peninsula on the shore side of the highway still bears the footprint of one of the most storied pioneer camps on the coast, where world-heavyweight-champion-to-be Jack Dempsey worked as a green chokerman in the early years of the century. The scraps of rusty logging equipment lying about date from more recent operations, and some of the dwellings scattered among the trees have a sameness of general shape that betrays their origin as camp buildings. BS&W closed their Myrtle Point site in 1926 and moved to even bigger things on Vancouver Island, but their early Powell River workings were one of the key pieces in building a forest empire that would bring them back to the area thirty-three years later—as co-owners of the Powell River pulp mill.

The experience of the people who settled south of town was much like that of people on the lower coast and coastal pioneers generally. They were lonely. They travelled half the day to visit a neighbour and a whole weekend to go to a dance. Without roads, boats became central players in the life, like the little steamboat nicknamed "Lopsided Lily," operated by "Steamboat Bob," which the logging companies used to hire to go down to the stumpranches and round up young ladies to entertain the boys at camp dances.

"We'd walk the nine miles down to the beach to go to the dance," remembered Lillian Palliser, whose unconventional English stepfather homesteaded inaccessible Horseshoe Valley above Stillwater. "Then we'd catch a boat to go over to Lang Bay...Stillwater had dances the odd time, and Myrtle Point. We had one fellow, a big Swede, Johnny Ulrich—and he played the music for all the dances...accordion, and boy, could he ever play! The drunker he got, the better he played."

Itinerant preachers and salesmen who came by boat, like the Rev. George Pringle on his *Sky Pilot* and radio expert Jim Spilsbury on the *Five BR*, were valued as much for their stories and good company as their services. The stories the oldtimers from this area tell tend to be grounded in weather and natural forces. Lillian Palliser recalled the dry summers that brought huge forest fires:

We were supposed to get out of the valley every year. Half the time we didn't do it, but this time the fire was right on us—you could see the flames of it. So Grampa went out and dug a great big hole in the garden, and

Mother took all her windows out of the house. She said if she had her windows, she could always build another house around them. We took all her windows and put them on top of all her stuff that she had: pots and pans and household stuff. It all went into this hole. Then dirt was put all over the top of it. Then Grampa walked right over it—broke half the windows.

If it wasn't fire it was snow or flooding rain, and if it wasn't that it was big winds, like the hurricane that broke up the Reverend Pringle's service at Lang Bay on January 29, 1921:

Big trees commenced to fall, crashing down on all sides of us. We had to shout into one another's ears to make ourselves heard. We were thankful to get to Smith's little frame house (where despite the storm, there was an overflow crowd). I announced a hymn. We were just getting the quavers out of our voices when the window tumbled in on my back. It took us fifteen minutes to get it nailed back and I was somewhere in "secondly" when a wild blast started the building paper lining the walls coming down, covering up my congregation...I didn't attempt to finish.

To survive in places like these you had to prize independence over almost every other trait. As you get nearer to Powell River proper however, the story changes. From the first days of the mill in 1911, the life Powell River offered was a highly regulated one, suited more to the type of person who was willing to endure shift work for a steady paycheque, something antithetical to the free-spirited settlers to the north and south of town. On top of this, Powell River was in its early days a total company town, where everything from the water you drank to the food you ate to the roof over your head was granted at the pleasure of the boss. It even had a store which was actually called "the Company Store." Grandfatherly old Dr. Dwight Brooks of the Brooks-Scanlon partnership was famous for the attention he paid to every detail of life in town and cast an atmosphere of benign but claustrophobic paternalism over all proceedings. The townsite school was called Brooks High School and a grand community centre was called Dwight Hall, after Dr. Brooks. Company managers were equally famous for

Operating continuously since 1911, the MacMillan Bloedel mill at Powell River has an annual capacity of 600,000 metric tonnes of paper, 52,000 short tons of pulp, 74 million board feet of lumber and employs 1,000.

handing out five-dollar bills to men whose wives had just given birth, and for blacklisting those who dared to question company policy.

It was very much to escape this absolute company rule that renegades began setting up pirate communities just outside the company pale, first around Cranberry Lake, then Wildwood—a favourite with Italian workers—and then the one that really took: Westview. By 1955 the company had acknowledged that its private kingdom had been superseded and sold off the townsite buildings. The *Powell River News* lamented, "Few better administered or generally happier company-controlled districts could be found in BC. Rents were low, there were no taxes for employees and all homes were maintained in first class repair. The 'Company Town Complex' was never evident in Powell River. Employees...look back with a degree of nostalgia to pre-1955 days."

Memories of what company town life was really like had to die down before nostalgia could blossom fully, but in recent years a vigorous restoration project has launched a campaign to restore and celebrate the old townsite, both the commercial section down by the mill and the residential section up on the hill above. It is one of those heritage sites whose importance is not so much in the quality of its architecture as in the history it represents. The guidebook *Sunshine and Salt Air* contains a good historical commentary on the townsite by local writer Karen Southern.

With the divestiture of the company-owned townsite, the separate villages of Cranberry Lake and Westview and the area of Wildwood were amalgamated with the old Powell River townsite to create the new Corporation of the District of Powell River. On the whole I have to agree with my dad about the results of this marriage. It did create a very vigorous, productive and at least outwardly contented community. Because the mill remained its central influence and focus, the combined community stayed unified after democratization, very much at odds with the anarchic style of the smaller logging and fishing villages of the *Baja* Sunshine Coast. Powell River people tend to mark off the periods of their lives not by timber claims they logged or fish boats they owned, but by the startup date of the first Kamyr digester or when the Number Seven Paper Machine shut down. Social relationships are influenced not by neighborhood so much as by mill shifts, as in "The Onderdonks lived just down the block but we never saw much of them because their men worked the 'A' shift and ours worked the 'B' shift."

The town never lacked for good community centres and it seethed with group activities. The largest ongoing feature in the community history *Pulp, Paper and People* by Karen Southern and Peggy Bird is one called "Clubs of the Decade," which follows the doings of groups like the Powell River Cricket Club, Powell River Pipe Band, Otago Rugby Club, and Women of the Moose. Community life centred on church activities, organized sports, social clubs and various artistic endeavours. As a bubble of ordered society surrounded by wilderness and isolated from any near neighbour, Powell River learned to be self-sufficient to the point of xenophobia. There was an "Us-Against-the-World" spirit which propelled participants to national and world class achievement in many areas.

In sports, Danny Lucas and Gary Lupul, products of the Powell River Minor Hockey Association, went on to play in the National Hockey League with the Philadelphia Flyers and the Vancouver Canucks. The Gerela brothers, Roy and Ted, made their name in pro football, Ted with the BC Lions and Roy with the Houston Oilers and Pittsburgh Steelers. Doug Ladret scored a top-ten finish in pairs figure skating competition at the 1988 Olympics.

The town's strong interest in the arts attracted talented instructors who began turning out star pupils. Ballet teacher Frieda Shaw saw one ex-pupil, Onna White, claim an Oscar for her choreography of the movie *Oliver* in 1969, while another, Norman Thompson, went on to become state director for the Vienna Opera House. Don Thompson graduated from Paul Daugherty's music classes to become Juno Award-winning jazz player. Silver Donald Cameron, whose educator father gave his name to Max Cameron High School, made his own name familiar across Canada as a bestselling journalist and author. The novelist and film writer Anne Cameron, who migrated to Powell River in the 1980s, exposes the dark side of mill - town life in her salty satires on the trials and triumphs of working class women, which are published around the world in many different languages. In commerce, Peter Toigo learned business basics helping his mom and pop run their Wildwood grocery store from the time he could see over the meat counter, subdivided a farm while he was still in high school, and went on to become one of the province's high-profile tycoons as owner of the White Spot Restaurant chain, among other holdings.

It is typical of Powell River that the activity which has spread its name farthest is one of the most communal of all—choral singing. Again it was the presence of an exceptional leader in the person of choirmaster Don James that led to the creation of several highly successful choirs. They won many awards performing in Germany, Poland, Mexico, England and the Soviet Union. Building on this success, in 1984 Powell River began hosting a biannual choral festival called Kathaumixw (Ka-thou-mew), a triumphant event that attracts people from all over the world. In the realm of international choral singing, Powell River is a Bayreuth or Salzburg.

Powell River author Anne Cameron's books about life in coastal mill towns are read all over the world.

Leaving Powell River and heading north, the story is pretty much a replay of the one to the south, except for the Sliammon Indian reserve just outside Wildwood. Sliammon offers no showpiece theatre-museum complex like its Sechelt counterpart, but the band is roughly equal in size and shares a similar history as a survivor of the Durieu system. Unlike Sechelt, the present Sliammon reserve is the Sliammon Band's traditional home, although it once shared winter quarters with the Klahoose and Homathco bands in Grace Harbour, a small bay in nearby Malaspina Inlet. Known as Kahkaykay, this winter meeting place must have been even more congested than Kalpalin.

Just north of Sliammon is an amorphous area known as Southview. The waterfront is peppered with residences and on the back land you can see scattered acreages dotted with skunk cabbage, marestail and the odd item of livestock that looks as if it would be happier wearing gumboots. The continental breadbasket it's not, though a few hardy stumpranchers like Mary Marsales supply a small but grateful following. You'd never hear it from her, but Mary once held the coastal record for oyster shucking.

TWENTY MILES NORTH OF POWELL RIVER is the village of Lund, a charming harbour community reminiscent of Egmont or Pender Harbour, with a small population of commercial fishboats and an interesting collection of character boats at the "guvvermint worf." Lund's glory is the Malaspina Hotel, a handsome turn-of-the-century structure that is probably the single most historic building left on the rural BC coast, now that some halfwit developer has torched the Minstrel Island Hotel. The Malaspina was built by Charles and Fredrick (Poppa) Thulin, two Swedish visionaries who founded the town of Lund in 1890, when their only company apart from the Texada towns would have been Leonard Frolander down at his Myrtle Point fur trading post, and possibly the unfortunate Jack Green, who officially opened his log cabin store on Savary Island in 1888.

Green is undisputed holder of the title of the first individual of European ancestry to be murdered on the Sunshine Coast, having been knocked on the head in 1893 by one Hugh Lynn, who subsequently became the first Sunshine Coast individual of any ancestry to be hanged by the neck. Green's game had been to offer provisions and small but very pricey snorts of firewater to the solitary handloggers who were working their way north by rowboat, looking for "stumpers"—jumbo fir trees overhanging the water that, when they were chopped down, would jump from the stump straight into the saltchuck.

By Thulins' time, the stumpers were all stumped and loggers were having to bring larger crews into the upcoast jungles to extract timber by oxen, horses and railroads. Their operations begat a stream of powerboat traffic funnelling into Calm Channel, and, the Thulins' plan was to offer steam towboats a last chance to get groceries, cordwood and larger but still pricey snorts of firewater before heading north into the Yaculta rapids, and it proved good business. Within a few years they had two hotels, three stores, a large steamer dock and their own very handsome but preposterously named towboat the *Niluht*.

Lund is listed in more trivia books than any town of its size in Canada owing to its position as the end of the road—the longest road in the world. There is a sign near the wharf noting that this is the northern terminus of Highway 101, a.k.a. the Pan American Highway, which begins in Terra del Fuego and ends here peering over the guardrail at the Lund gas dock. A small but very dedicated movement convenes every night in the Malaspina Hotel bar (and all day on Saturdays) for the purpose of reversing the Pan American Highway so the end would be in Chile and Lund would have the beginning. I never miss a session without regretting it. There is no better place to lay

over a bit and ponder the history that has streamed through the venerable Malaspina portals in the course of the century, the loafers and the muckers in pursuit of their contrary obsessions, modifying this sometimes sunshiney tract of real estate as they went, smudging its beauty here and there but finally posing only an indifferent challenge to its magnificence.

In his pensive 1932 novella *The Western Wall*, Hubert Evans pronounced what could be the final word on those restless seekers, loafers and muckers both. Now that their search for different ways has fetched them up against this wall of western ocean, he wrote, drawing them together in the realization that there is nowhere further to go, they must finally turn and face the task of forging a livable world together. Sometimes, as I eavesdrop on the fishermen at the next table squabbling over the allocation of the last few beleagured coho, I am not sure Hubert's caveat is coming any closer to realization. Then, when I listen to the snaggle-toothed old logger on the other side of me say he's got so used to the new look in the woods it seems completely natural to pick up his sandwich wrappings and pack them out of the bush in his lunchbucket, I think maybe we are.

The spirit of the pioneers that hovers over the Malaspina bar makes such reflections unavoidable, though in the pleasantest possible way. A session there also has the quite magical effect, that whenever the travellers decide it is done, early or late, and once again mount the steps up to that incredibly long, incredibly winding road, they will discover it has indeed reversed itself, and a new opportunity to explore the Sunshine Coast in its endless diversity waits to begin.

Opposite:

On a day half drizzle, half fog
an eagle swims above weedy trees
the sun explodes like a bomb
the teeth of the wind are keen with winter
We are several snowfalls from spring.
The day is a two-faced coin
the mist hangs thick on the earth's edge
the rest: blue glisten, green candour.

Peter Trower, "Two Phantoms in January"

Freil Lake Falls in Hotham Sound are admired by thousands of passengers who annually take the Powell River ferry between Saltery Bay and Earl's Cove.

When they hear the name Powell River, most outsiders think only of a huge pulp mill belching fumes, but the area possesses some of the best scenery on the BC coast. Here community's fleet of pleasure craft rests at Westview basin.

One underwater area in Thunder Bay near Powell River has such a well-established octopus population divers have nicknamed it "Octopus City."

Townsfolk crowd Willingdon Beach for a look at Coast Guard hovercraft during Powell River Seafair.

Left: One of the area's favourite playgrounds is Powell Lake (left).

Below left: Water lilies on Cranberry Lake are sometimes harvested commercially.

Cranberry Pottery in Cranberry Lake neighborhood is a must-see for collectors of fine hand-made pottery.

Below: Originally a company town built in the shadow of the big pulpmill, the old Powell River townsite is being restored as a heritage area. This handsome building is known as "The Old Courthouse."

Above: The Powell Forest, one of the best coniferous growing areas in Canada, is coming back in dense second growth after being logged earlier in the century.

Below left: Longtime Powell River residents Charlie and Gerri Parsons are strong advocates of the "small is beautiful" approach to the forest industry. Here they demonstrate a portable sawmill.

Below right: Powell Riverites relive logging history with an antique two-man chainsaw at Seafair celebrations.

Above: Powell River's loggers, like those on the lower coast, have had to adapt to shrinking timber supplies. As timber harvesting focuses on the less accessible stands on high elevations, helicopter logging becomes a practical method for transporting logs.

Right: A traditional logging operation unloads a truck at Powell Lake.

The names we inflict on mountains
bounce meaninglessly away —
the mountains know who they are.
The earth forbears our nibblings
our ant strivings, ignores
the itch of our presumptions.

Peter Trower, "The Presumers"

Top: Mother rufous hummingbird with nestlings.

Above: Saw-whet owl.

Weathered snags on mountain known as "The Knuckleheads."

Below: The mountainous area inland from Powell River offers spectacular alpine scenery. Here hikers admire view of Daniel Lake.

Top: Quarries on Texada Island have long been one of the province's leading sources of industrial limestone. Mineral wealth made Texada the Sunshine Coast's first developed area.

Above: Tug manoeuvres bargeload of limestone at Blubber Bay, Texada Island.

Its days as a whaling centre far behind it, Blubber Bay is third in rank among Texada Island communities, following Vananda and Gillies Bay. Island population has fallen since closure of large iron mine near Gillies Bay, and now hovers near 1,000.

Texada Island—Powell River Ferry North Island Princess *brings another cargo of commuters and shoppers into Blubber Bay.*

One of the more exotic of the Gulf Islands, Savary has long been one of the coast's best popular holiday spots.

Killer whales (Orcinus orca) are a common sight in Sunshine Coast waters. Individuals can be distinguished by the unique characteristics of their dorsal fins.

Boat travel becomes second nature to upcoast kids.

This giant arbutus tree on the south side of Savary Island is reputedly the largest in the world.

Everything Savary Islanders need has to be shipped out of Lund by boat—even cars.

Aerial view of Lund. Lund was founded in 1890 by Charles and Frederick (Poppa) Thulin, two Swedish visionaries who saw the need for an upcoast depot to service towboats and loggers. It continues today as a boating centre and fishing village of 1200 people.

Below: The boat basin at Lund shelters a clourful collection of commercial work boats and barnacled liveaboards.

Old waterwheel on Lund boardwalk.

Below: The Malaspina Hotel in Lund dates back to the 1800s.

Bottom: Two ways of looking at the matter.

Published with the assistance of the Canada Council and the Cultural Services Branch of the BC Government
by Harbour Publishing Co. Ltd. P.O. Box 219, Madeira Park, B.C. V0N 2H0.

Edited by Mary Schendlinger
Designed by Roger Handling, Terra Firma Design
Front cover photograph by Keith Thirkell
Back cover photograph by Dean vantSchip

Printed and bound in Canada by Friesen Printers

ACKNOWLEDGEMENTS

This book would not have been possible but for the remarkable pool of photographic talent that exists on the Sunshine Coast. Keith Thirkell led the way and Ken Bell, Mary Cain, Tim Poole, Tim Turner and Dean vantSchip made major contributions. Carole Bowes, Paul Galinski, Charlaine Lacroix, Jim Willoughby added essential pieces. I was moved by the participation of artists Britton Francis, Greta Guzek, Gaye Hammond, June Malaka, Jan Poynter, April White and Jim Willer. The aerial photographs taken by Keith Thirkell appear courtesy Fleetwood Forest Products and Sechelt Gibsons Air, who generously provided flying time. Boat travel was kindly provided by superguide John DaFoe. I am indebted to Candy Clarke, Theresa Jeffries, Ann Quinn, Karen Southern, and Brin Wilson for their expert suggestions on the manuscript. This book is dedicated to my dad, Frank White, a builder of the Sunshine Coast.

ISBN 1-55017-081-3

Canadian Cataloguing in Publication Data

White, Howard, 1945–
   The Sunshine Coast

   1. Sunshine Coast (B.C.) – Description and travel. 2. Sunshine
Coast (B.C.) – History. I. Title
FC3845.S95W54 1996   971.1'31   C94-910171-0
F1089.S95W54 1996

PHOTO CREDITS

Numbers indicate page, letters indicate height on page (A=top). **Ken Bell**: 9a, 16, 20a, 32b, 32c, 33, 34b, 37a, 52c, 56a, 97b.
Carole Bowes: 123a. **Mary Cain**: 5a, 34c, 64-65, 66a, 76c, 77, 78b, 81a, 81b, 84c, 85, 86c, 88-89, 90a, 90b, 93a, 110a.
Elphinstone Pioneer Museum: 10, 20b. **Roger Handling**: 49. **Charlaine Lacroix**: 76b.
Tim Poole: 114a, 116a, 116b, 117a, 117b,123b.
Poole-Galinski Photography Inc.: 5c, 96, 97a, 100-101, 106, 108, 120a, 120b, 122a.
Keith Thirkell: 1, 2-3, 4a, 4b, 4c, 8a, 8b, 11a, 11b, 12, 18-19, 21, 22, 23, 27, 30a, 30b, 31b, 32a, 34a, 35a, 35b, 36a, 36b, 37b,
38-39, 40a, 40b, 40c, 41a, 41b, 42-43, 44, 46, 50, 52a, 52b, 53a, 53b, 54-55, 56b, 56c, 57a, 57b, 57c, 58a, 58b, 59a, 59b,
60a, 60-61, 62a, 62b, 62c, 63, 66b, 70, 72, 76a, 78a, 79a, 79b, 79c, 80a, 80b, 82-83, 84a, 84b, 86b, 87a, 87b, 93b, 94, 102b,
104, 107, 110b, 111a, 111b, 112a, 112b, 113a, 113b, 114b, 114c, 115a, 115b, 118a, 118b, 119a, 119b, 121a, 121c, 122b, 123c.
Tim Turner: 13, 30-31. **Dean vantSchip**: 4-5, 5b, 32c, 45, 61a, 61b, 98-99, 121b. **April White**: 14-15. **Howard White**: 86a.
Jim Willoughby: 103, 111a.

FURTHER READING ON THE SUNSHINE COAST

Alsgard, A.H., *Powell River's First 50 Years*, Powell River News, Powell River, 1960.

Bradley, R. Ken, *Historic Railways of the Powell River Area*, B.C. Railway Historical Association, Victoria, 1982.

Calhoun, Bruce, *Mac and the Princess: The Story of Princess Louisa Inlet*, Ricwalt Publishing, Seattle, 1976.

Cameron, Anne, *A Whole Brass Band*, Harbour Publishing, Madeira Park, 1994.

Cameron, Anne, *Selkie*, Harbour Publishing, Madeira Park, 1996.

Cameron, Anne, *The Whole Fam Damily*, Harbour Publishing, Madeira Park, 1995.

Carson, Bryan et al, *Sunshine and Salt Air: A Recreation Guide to the Sunshine Coast*, Harbour Publishing, Madeira Park, 1991 and 1997.

Dawe, Helen *Helen Dawe's Sechelt*, Harbour Publishing, Madeira Park, 1990.

Evans, Hubert, *Mostly Coast People*, Harbour Publishing, Madeira Park, 1982.

Graham, Donald, *Lights of the Inside Passage: A history of BC's Lightouses and Their Keepers*, Harbour Publishing, 1986.

Hammond, Dick, *Tales From Hidden Basin*, Harbour Publishing, Madeira Park, 1996.

Hill-Tout, Charles, *The Salish People Vol. IV: The Sechelt and the South Eastern Tribes of Vancouver Island*, Talonbooks, Vancouver, 1978.

Iglauer, Edith, *Fishing With John*, Harbour Publishing, Madeira Park, 1988.

Keller, Betty C., and Leslie, Rosella, *Bright Seas, Pioneer Spirits: The Sunshine Coast*, Horsdal & Schubart 1996.

Kennedy, Dorothy and Bouchard, Randy, *Sliammon Life, Sliammon Lands*, Talonbooks, Vancouver, 1983.

Kennedy, Ian *Sunny Sandy Savary: A history of Savary Island 1792-1992*, Kennell Publishing, Vancouver, 1992.

Mason, Elda Copley, *Lasqueti Island: History and Memory*, Byron Mason, Lantzville, 1975.

McIntyre, Margaret, *Place of Quiet Waters*, Longmans Canada, Don Mills, 1965

Peterson, Lester *The Gibsons Landing Story*, Peter Martin Books Canada 1962.

Peterson, Lester, *The Story of the Sechelt Nation*, Harbour Publishing, Madeira Park, 1990.

Roberts Creek Historical Society, *Remembering Roberts Creek 1889-1955*, Harbour Publishing, Madeira Park, 1978.

Roberts, Harry, *The Trail of Chack Chack*, Carlton, New York 1968

Rubin, Dan, *Salt on the Wind: The Sailing Life of Allen and Sharie Farrell*, Horsdal and Schubart, 1996.

Schweizer, W. H. *Beyond Understanding: The Complete Guide to Princess Louisa Inlet, Chatterbox Falls, Jervis Inlet* EOS Publishing, Seattle 1989

Sinclair, B.W. *Poor Man's Rock*, Little Brown, New York, 1920.

Smart, Elizabeth, *By Grand Central Station I Sat Down and Wept*, Deneau Publishers, Ottawa, 1981.

Southern, Karen, and Bird, Peggy, *Pulp, Paper and People: 75 Years of Powell River*, Powell River Heritage Research Association, Powell River, 1990.

Southern, Karen, *The Nelson Island Story*, Hancock House, Surrey, 1987.

Spilsbury, Jim, *Spilsbury's Album*, Harbour Publishing, Madeira Park, 1987.

Thompson, Bill, *Boats, Bucksaws and Blisters: Pioneer Tales of the Powell River Area*, Powell River Heritage Research Association, Powell River,1993.

Thompson, Bill, *Once Upon A Stump: Times and Tales of Powell River Pioneers*, Powell River Heritage Research Association, Powell River, 1993.

Trower, Peter, *Bush Poems*, Harbour Publishing, Madeira Park, 1978.

Trower, Peter, *Grogan's Cafe*, Harbour Publishing, Madeira Park, 1995.

Trower, Peter, *Ragged Horizons*, McClelland and Stewart, Toronto, 1978.

Twigg, Alan, *Hubert Evans: The First Ninety-Three Years*, Harbour Publishing, Madeira Park, 1985.

White, Howard and Spilsbury, Jim, *Spilsbury's Coast*, Harbour Publishing, Madeira Park, 1987.

White, Howard and Spilsbury, Jim, *The Accidental Airline*, Harbour Publishing, Madeira Park, 1988.

White, Howard, Ed. *Raincoast Chronicles First Five*, Harbour Publishing, Madeira Park.

White, Howard, Ed. *Raincoast Chronicles Six-Ten*, Harbour Publishing, Madeira Park.

White, Howard, Ed., *Raincoast Chronicles Eleven Up*, Harbour Publishing, Madeira Park.

White, Howard, *Ghost in the Gears*, Harbour Publishing, Madeira Park, 1993.

White, Howard, *The Men There Were Then*, Arsenal Pulp Press, Vancouver, 1983.

White, Howard, *Writing in the Rain*, Harbour Publishing, Madeira Park, 1990.

White, Stewart Edward, *Skookum Chuck*, Garden City, New York 1925.

INDEX

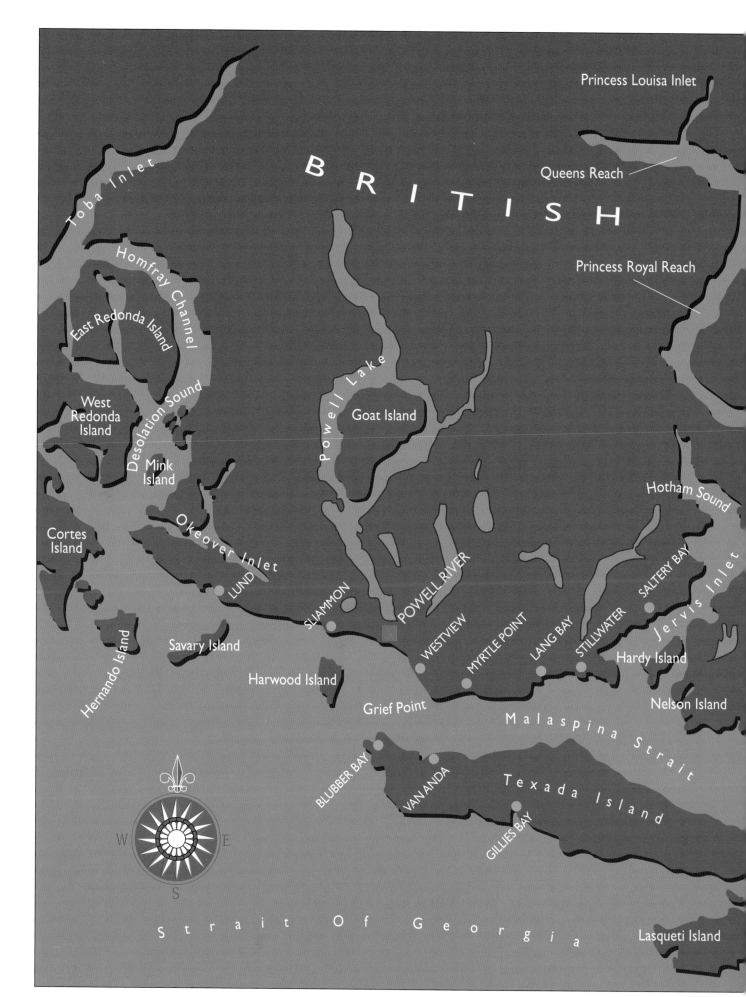